The HIDDEN PLACES *of* CORNWALL

including the Isles of Scilly

Edited by
Barbara Vesey

Published by:
Travel Publishing Ltd
7a Apollo House, Calleva Park
Aldermaston, Berks, RG7 8TN

ISBN 1-902-00713-1

First Published: *1989*
Second Edition: *1992*
Third Edition: *1996*
Fourth Edition: *1998*

Regional Titles in the Hidden Places Series:

Channel Islands
Cheshire
Cornwall
Devon
Dorset, Hants & Isle of Wight
Gloucestershire
Heart of England
Kent
Lake District & Cumbria
Lancashire
Norfolk
Northeast Yorkshire
Northumberland & Durham
Nottinghamshire
Peak District
Potteries
Somerset
South East
South Wales
Suffolk
Surrey
Sussex
Thames & Chilterns
Welsh Borders
Wiltshire
Yorkshire Dales

National Titles in the Hidden Places Series:

England
Ireland
Scotland
Wales

Printing by: Nuffield Press, Abingdon
Cartography by: Estates Publications, Tenterden, Kent
Line Drawings: Sarah Bird
Editor: Barbara Vesey
Cover : Clare Hackney

Born in 1961, Clare was educated at West Surrey College of Art and Design as well as studying at Kingston University. She runs her own private water-colour school based in Surrey and has exhibited both in the UK and internationally. The cover is taken from an original water-colour of the cliffs around Land's End.

Foreword

The Hidden Places series is a collection of easy to use travel guides taking you, in this instance, on a relaxed but informative tour through the county of Cornwall, an area of outstanding natural beauty. In the final chapter we have also included some information on the Isles of Scilly due to its close proximity. Our books contain a wealth of interesting information on the history, the countryside, the towns and villages and the more established places of interest in the county. But they also promote the more secluded and little known visitor attractions and places to stay, eat and drink many of which are easy to miss unless you know exactly where you are going.

We include hotels, inns, restaurants, public houses, teashops, various types of accommodation, historic houses, museums, gardens, garden centres, craft centres and many other attractions throughout the county of Cornwall. Most places have an attractive line drawing and are cross-referenced to coloured maps found at the rear of the book. We do not award merit marks or rankings but concentrate on describing the more interesting, unusual or unique features of each place with the aim of making the reader's stay in the local area an enjoyable and stimulating experience.

Whether you are visiting the area for business or pleasure or in fact are living in the county we do hope that you enjoy reading and using this book. We are always interested in what readers think of places covered (or not covered) in our guides so please do not hesitate to use the reader reaction forms provided to give us your considered comments. We also welcome any general comments which will help us improve the guides themselves. Finally if you are planning to visit any other corner of the British Isles we would like to refer you to the list of other ***Hidden Places*** titles to be found at the rear of the book.

Contents

CHAPTER ONE
Northeast Cornwall

Tintagel Castle

Chapter 1 - Area Covered

For precise location of places please refer to the colour maps found at the rear of the book.

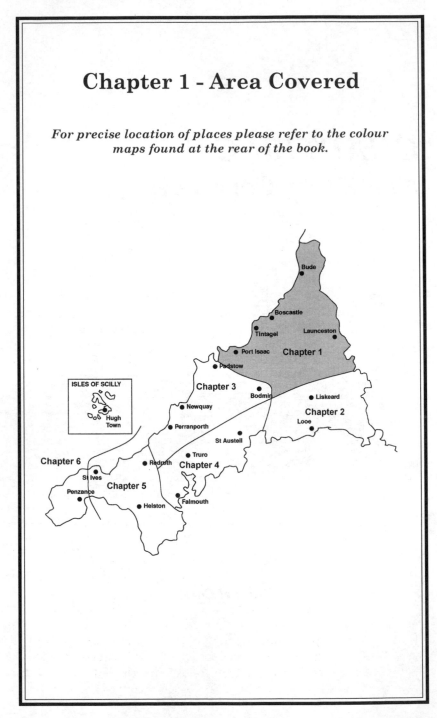

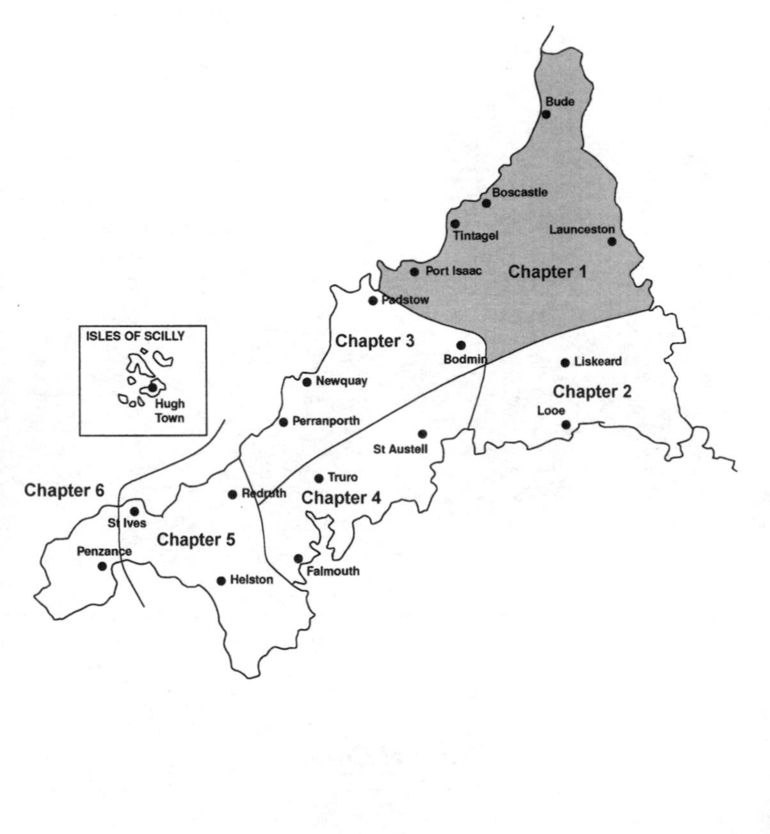

1
Northeast Cornwall

Introduction

Separated from the rest of mainland Britain by the River Tamar, which rises just behind the north coast to the northeast of Bude, and forms the boundary with Devon, this part of Cornwall, like the rest, is plentiful in small villages of granite houses and narrow, winding lanes. The natural barrier of the Tamar has, over the centuries, preserved Cornwall's Celtic heritage - still very much in evidence today. Place names beginning with *Tre*, *Pol* and *Pen* are the most common reminders. Others are the many ancient remains of crosses, holy wells and prehistoric sites throughout the countryside.

The northeastern area of Cornwall is dominated by the bleak expanse of ***Bodmin Moor***, which covers some 80 square miles. The two highest peaks on the exposed moorland both lie here in the north: the 1,370-foot ***Brown Willy*** and, almost as high, ***Rough Tor***. More evidence of early occupation can be seen between the A30 and ***Hawks Tor***, the site of a Neolithic henge monument known as the ***Stripple Stones***. This area of Cornwall is also home to ***The Cheesewring***, a spectacular natural granite formation. There are also a great many reminders of the presence of Roman and Norman occupation.

Northeast Cornwall is renowned for its fine dairy products (especially cheeses), and has many connections with the author Thomas Hardy and the poet John Betjeman. And while nowhere in Cornwall is more than 20 miles from the sea, the northeast coast is unique in many respects. Particularly around Boscastle and Tintagel, this is a landscape dominated by high cliffs. Of course the sea has always played an important part in life in the villages of Cornwall - in addition to fishing and trawling, dealing in contraband was once a common way of supplementing income, as the coastline offers many convenient hiding places expansive enough to accommodate even the largest haul of ill-gotten goods.

Launceston

Launceston (the local pronunciation is *Lawn-son*) is one of the most pleasant inland towns in Cornwall. For centuries it was an important regional capital which guarded the main overland route into the county. Shortly after the Norman invasion, William the Conqueror's half-brother, Robert of Mortain, built a massive ***Castle*** here on an elevated site above the River Kensey. From this castle fort, subsequent Earls of Cornwall tried to govern the fiercely independent Cornish people. A fine example of a motte and bailey castle, the outer bailey is now a public park; there is also a round double keep, the outer walls of which are 12 foot thick in places. Also in its time used as a gaol, where prisoners were kept in appalling conditions in this decaying fortress, its inmates included founder of the Quakers, George Fox.

Launceston Castle

Launceston boasts a number of fine old buildings and churches. In medieval times a settlement grew up around an Augustinian priory on the northern side of the River Kensey. It is here that the original parish ***Church of St Stephen*** stands. Nearby there is a Byzantine-style Roman Catholic church, built early in the 20th century. The oldest surviving ecclesiastical building in the town is the 12th century ***Church of St Thomas***, near the southern end of the medieval footbridge that crosses the river - surprisingly, within this tiny building stands the largest Norman font in Cornwall.

Some of the most impressive stonework in the area is used in the ***Church of St Mary Magdelene***, a 16th century granite structure built by a local landowner after the tragic death of his wife and son. He assembled the finest stonemasons in Cornwall to create, in their memory, a remarkable cornucopia of ornamental carving which covers nearly every surface of the building.

Elsewhere in Launceston, the streets around the castle are filled with handsome buildings dating from Georgian times and earlier, including the National Trust-owned ***Lawrence House*** in Castle Street. Housing an interesting town museum, this was built in 1753 and contains some fine plasterwork ceilings. The art gallery near the medieval ***South Gate***, the only remaining vestige of Launceston's town walls, is also worth a visit. To the west of the town, a ***Steam***

Launceston Steam Railway

Railway runs along the Kensey valley. Other nearby attractions include ***Tamar Otter Park*** and ***Trethorne Leisure Farm***.

Three Steps to Heaven is a charming and very attractive restaurant brimming with atmosphere. In close proximity to all the sites both in Launceston itself (the castle ruins and the town's museum, to name but two) and in the surrounding coastal and inland areas, the restaurant is actually part of the town's Southgate Archway. It features a handsome 19th century stone and slate exterior

Three Steps to Heaven

and a warm and cosy interior decorated with Guinness memorabilia (co-owners Simon Walsh and Estelle Daligaux are collectors) and features simple, attractive furnishings and soft lighting in the main dining area. Simon is also the chef, and brings 10 years' experience in catering to the original and classic menu, while his partner Estelle runs the front of house with grace and efficiency. The menu makes the most of fresh ingredients - locally produced fish, seafood and country vegetables - and is all home-cooked and home-prepared. Apart from a changing selection of daily specials, the menu boasts steak, pasta, chicken, pork, beef and vegetable dishes, for both lunch and dinner. Closed Sunday night and Mondays. *Three Steps to Heaven, 1 Southgate Place, Launceston, Cornwall PL15 8BS Tel: 01566 775748.*

Around Launceston

North Petherwin — *Map 3 ref O4*

4 miles NW of Launceston off the B3254

North Petherwin is the location of ***Tamar Otter Park***, a fascinating place offering the chance to see otters and other wildlife in their natural habitat.

Egloskerry — *Map 3 ref O5*

2 miles NW of Launceston off the A395

The impressive manor house of ***Penheale*** in Egloskerry was home in the 17th century to the influential Speccott family, many of whom are memorialised at the part-Norman church.

Laneast — *Map 3 ref N5*

7 miles W of Launceston off the A395

The part-Norman church in Laneast contains an impressive rood screen, some striking 15th century carved bench ends, and a pair of graceful wagon roofs in the south aisle and the south porch. The parish of Laneast was the birthplace of John Adams, the astronomer who first discovered the planet Neptune. A small chapel to the southeast of the church stands over a holy well, one of many such springs to be found in this part of Cornwall.

St Clether — *Map 3 ref N5*

7 miles W of Launceston off the A395

An elaborate holy well can be found a few hundred yards northwest of this tranquil village, standing on its own on a bracken-covered shelf above the River Inney. With its adjacent 15th century chapel, this well is the most enchanting of its kind in the county. The village itself has a part-Norman church which was heavily restored by the Victorians; however, a number of earlier features have survived, including the Norman stone pillars and font and the 15th century tower..

Altarnun — *Map 3 ref N5*

7½ miles SW of Launceston off the A30

This charming Bodmin Moor village lies in the steep-sided valley of ***Penpont Water***. It features a 15th century packhorse bridge and outstanding, largely 15th century parish church standing in a superb position on a rise above the peat-stained river. Sometimes referred to as the *'Cathedral of the Moors'*, this surprisingly grand moorstone structure is dedicated to St Nonna, the mother of St David, patron saint of Wales. It has a tall pinnacled tower and an unusually light and spacious interior which contains a carved rood screen, a decorated Norman font and a wonderful series of over 70 Tudor bench ends whose carvings create a charming picture of 16th century village life.

In the churchyard there are several fine examples of the work of Altarnun-born sculptor Nevill Northey Bunard, who carved the bust of John Wesley which stands over the door of the Meeting House by the stream.

Upton Cross — *Map 3 ref O6*

8 miles S of Launceston off the B3254

This handsome village is home to ***Sterts Art Centre***. As well as a gallery, dance studio and cafe, it boasts one of the few open-air amphitheatres in the country.

Bodmin Moor

The bleak expanse of Bodmin Moor stretches either side of the A30. This 80 square-mile area of granite upland is characterised by saturated moorland and weather-beaten tors. The exposed area to the north of the main road supports the 1,377-foot hill known as ***Brown Willy***, the highest point in Cornwall.

Bodmin Moor

Almost as high, and standing on National Trust-owned land a bit to the northwest, is ***Rough Tor***, a magnificent viewpoint which is also the site of a memorial to the men of the Wessex Regiment killed in the Second World War. This dramatic area of the moor is best approached from the northwest along the lane leading up from the A39 at Camelford.

Like Dartmoor, Bodmin Moor is covered in prehistoric remains. Typical of many are the scattered Bronze Age hut circles and field enclosures which can be seen on the side of Rough Tor. Slightly south of this lies the ***Fernacre Stone Circle***. Also Bronze Age, it contains more than 30 standing stones and is the largest of this kind of structure on the Moor.

Evidence of even earlier occupation can be found between the A30 and ***Hawks Tor***, the site of a Neolithic henge monument known as the ***Stripple Stones***.

Within Bodmin Moor

Minions — *Map 3 ref O7*

9 miles SW of Launceston off the B3254

Here in this exposed former mining community, on the southeastern fringe of Bodmin Moor, stands ***Hurlers Stone Circle***, an impressive Bronze Age temple consisting of three stone circles arranged in a line. According to Cornish legend, the circles were formed when teams of local men were turned to stone for hurling (playing the game that is a Celtic form of hockey) on the Sabbath.

Half a mile away to the north stands the spectacular natural granite formation known as ***The Cheesewring***. Another local legend has it that this was the haunt of a druid who possessed a golden chalice which never ran dry and provided thirsty passersby with and endless supply of water. The story was partially borne out in 1818 when archaeologists excavating a nearby burial chamber discovered a skeleton clutching a golden cup - dubbed the Rillaton Cup, it is now in the British Museum. The lovely ***Siblyback Reservoir*** is less than two miles west of Minions.

Henwood — *Map 3 ref O6*

8 miles SW of Launceston off the B3254

Henwood Barns Holiday Cottages are three picturesque, comfortable and well-equipped holiday homes located in the peaceful village of Henwood, on the edge of Bodmin Moor between Launceston

Henwood Barns Holiday Cottages

and Liskeard. Conveniently based for all kinds of holiday pursuits, these three 18th century converted barns are set around the original farmyard. Henwood Barn sleeps six, Small Barn four, and cosy Mole Cottage accommodates two. Each has a wood-burning stove and remains in keeping with the buildings' original character yet is equipped with every modern convenience. There are stunning views over the surrounding countryside, up to the Moor beyond. Henwood village is a conservation area, tucked into a small valley and sheltered by the peaks of Sharptor and the Cheesewring.

The surrounding countryside is a designated area of outstanding natural beauty. Walkers will find no end of scenic and interesting rambles in the area; Liskeard, nearby, has many welcome amenities, there is a watersports centre at hand at Siblyback Lake, and the coast is only 15 miles away - making this an ideal location from which to explore the natural beauty and tranquillity of this part of Cornwall. *Roseland Cottage, Henwood, Liskeard, Cornwall PL14 5BP Tel: 01579 363576.*

Bolventor — *Map 3 ref N6*

10 miles SW of Launceston off the A30

Midway between Launceston and Bodmin in the centre of the Moor, this scenic village is the location of the former coaching inn which was immortalised in Daphne du Maurier's novel, *Jamaica Inn.* During the 18th and 19th centuries, this isolated hostelry provided an ideal meeting-place for outlaws and smugglers; something of its former atmosphere lives on despite its modern role as a haven for passing motorists.

A lane south of Bolventor leads past the mysterious natural tarn known as ***Dozmary Pool***, another place which is ensconced in Cornish legend. According to one tale, King Arthur was brought here following his final battle at Slaughter Bridge, near Camelford. As he lay dying at the water's edge, he implored Sir Bedivere to throw his mystical sword, Excalibur, into the centre of the lake. The reluctant knight did so, and as the sword flew through the air towards the water, the disembodied hand of the Lady of the Lake rose out of the water to catch it.

Although the tarn is rumoured to be bottomless, cattle can sometimes be seen wading near its centre - and, indeed, it purportedly dried up completely during the prolonged drought of 1869.

Dozmary Pool is also said to be one of the many places in Cornwall which is haunted by Jan Tregeagle, the wicked steward of the Earl of Radnor whose many evil deeds including the murder of the parents of a young child whose estate he wanted to get his hands on. As a punishment, he was condemned to spend eternity emptying the lake using only a limpet shell with a hole in it.

Just south of Dozmary Pool the road passes alongside ***Colliford Reservoir***, a man-made lake which offers some excellent recreational and watersports facilities.

St Neot

Map 3 ref N7

12½ miles SW of Launceston off the B3254

This tranquil community lies a couple of miles downstream of Colliford Dam. The village is named after the diminutive 9th century saint who spent a large part of his life immersed up to his neck in the holy well which lies a couple of hundred yards upstream from the church. According to local folklore, the pool was also occupied by a fish which would be caught and eaten every day, only to reappear miraculously next morning to start the process all over again.

Episodes from the life of St Neot are depicted in the magnificent stained-glass windows of the ***parish church***, a handsome 15th century structure with a 14th century tower. Thought to be one of the finest collections of early stained glass in Cornwall, the windows also show a selection of delicately-fashioned scenes from the Old Testament.

Warleggan

Map 3 ref N7

12½ miles SW of Launceston off the A30

A steep lane rises through the woods towards this remote hamlet on the southern margins of Bodmin Moor. This settlement has long been associated with the supernatural, and is an acknowledged haunt of the Cornish *'piskies'*.

Warleggan's most eccentric resident, however, was a spiritual practitioner of quite another stripe: the Reverend Frederick Densham was parish priest in 1931, when he came to the hamlet and immediately succeeded in alienating his flock by closing the Sunday school, erecting barbed wire around the rectory and bringing in a pack of German Shepherd dogs to patrol the grounds! The parishioners responded by staying away in droves, to the extent that one entry in the parish register of the time reads, *'No fog. No wind. No rain. No congregation.'* To compensate, the Revd Densham fashioned cardboard replicas of the church rectors, placed them in the pews, and preached on. There is also evidence of Densham's kinder nature, however: he constructed a children's playground in the rectory garden.

Cardinham *Map 2 ref M7*

15 miles SW of Launceston off the A30

A number of Celtic standing stones are scattered throughout the parish of Cardinham, on the outskirts southwest of Bodmin Moor, including one in the churchyard which is inscribed in Latin. The churchyard is also the setting for a richly decorated 10th century cross which is over 8 feet tall.

Cardinham contains relics from almost every era in Cornwall's history. The church is dedicated to the little-known hermit, St Meubred. It dates from the 15th century and contains some impressive wagon roofs, a Norman font, a set of carved bench ends, and a rare early 15th century monumental brass depicting a life-size figure of Thomas Awmarle.

Today a peaceful backwater with the scenic ***Cardinham Woods***, excellent for cyclists and walkers, in medieval times Cardinham was the location of an important Norman motte and bailey castle belonging to the Cardinham family, under-lords of Robert of Mortain of Launceston. The structure was abandoned in the 14th century; today only an earthwork mound remains on which a few traces over the original keep have been preserved.

Blisland *Map 2 ref M6*

15 miles SW of Launceston off the A30

This lovely village lies hidden in the maze of country lanes which criss-cross the western margins of Bodmin Moor. At the centre of the village stands a broad, tree-lined green which retains its original Saxon plan, an uncommon feature on this side of the River Tamar.

The green is bordered by some exceptional Georgian and Victorian buildings, including a manor house, rectory, school, forge and inn.

The bright whitewashed interior of the part-Norman ***Church of St Protus and St Hyacinth*** was a favourite of Sir John Betjeman, who described it as *'dazzling and amazing'*. It has a good wagon roof, an unusual mock-Renaissance altar and some impressive monuments and tombs.

St Tudy

Map 2 ref M6

15 miles W of Launceston off the A39

At the heart of this scattered village stands another fine church. Mainly 15th century, it has a rare Norman font made of Purbeck marble and some remarkably detailed monuments to 16th and 17th century members of the Nicholls family. Just the other side of the A39 is home to the ***Cornwall Donkey and Pony Sanctuary***.

Bude

Bude, with its sweeping expanse of sand and Atlantic breakers rolling in from the west, seems to change its character with every change in the weather - a winter gale can make it seem like a remote outpost clinging to the edge of the world, while a warm summer breeze transforms it into a genial holiday town with some excellent facilities for beach-lovers, surfers and coastal walkers. It enjoys its status as a prime north coast resort with find sandy beaches, rock pools, and tidal swimming pool.

Belinda's Restaurant & Coffee Shop

While exploring the delights of the town, visitors might like to stop in at ***Belinda's Restaurant and Coffee Shop*** a cheerful and welcoming establishment located just off the main high street, on the corner of Princes Street. This lively family restaurant offers delicious snacks and meals - all of which make the most of fresh produce locally produced and prepared on site. Specialities include pasta dishes and pizzas. Very popular with walkers and holiday-makers, and open every day during the busy summer season, this crisp, clean restaurant calls to mind an Italian-style bistro with its marbled counter and table-tops, simple black and white interior and varnished exposed stone walls, handsomely festooned with hanging plants. The atmosphere is vivacious and convivial; proprietors Paul and Belinda Coe do their utmost to make any visit to this comfortable and homely establishment pleasant and memorable. *Belinda's Restaurant and Coffee Shop, 8 Princes Street, Bude, Cornwall EX23 8LT Tel: 01288 352294.*

Bude's late-Victorian and Edwardian centre is sheltered from the worst Atlantic extremes by a low cliff which separates the shallow valley of the River Neet from the ocean.

Another charming place to enjoy some well-earned refreshment is ***Morwenna***, a licensed cafe, bakery and take-away situated at the top of the high street in Bude. With its slate roof, cream-coloured exterior and picturesque awnings over the large windows, it is the quintessential cosy and welcoming cafe. The extensive interior boasts bench-style seating; the large sun terrace on the paved area in front is the perfect place to enjoy tea and refreshments in warmer weather. Very popular all year round, Morwenna's excellent menu is wide ranging, and includes all-day breakfast, vegetarian dishes, snacks, lunches (from beefburgers to curries), Cornish cream teas and a special children's menu. The cafe is (justly) famous for its pasties, made to a secret recipe originally created by two local school dinner-ladies. A visit to this lively and friendly establishment is a treat worth seeking out. *Morwenna Restaurant, 2 Morwenna Terrace, Bude, Cornwall EX23 8BU Tel: 01288 356600.*

Morwenna Cafe

The town stood at the northern end of the now-disused ***Bude Canal***, an ambitious early-19th century inland waterway which was intended to connect the Atlantic with the English Channel by way of the River Tamar. The only stretch to be completed, that between Bude and Launceston, was largely used for transporting seaweed, sand and other fertilisers to inland farms. Abandoned when the railway arrived in the 1890's, the two mile long section at the northern end has now been restored for use as a recreational amenity. The small fort guarding the northern entrance to the canal was built in the 1840's as an eccentric private residence, and the old forge on the canalside has been converted into an interesting ***Museum*** exploring Bude's maritime heritage. The ***Bude-Stratton Historical Folk Exhibition***, also on the canal, and the ***World of Nature*** in the town centre, are two more fascinating places to visit. Bude is also host to an Annual Jazz Festival every summer.

Crooklets Road, leading northwest of the town, takes visitors to ***Maer Lodge***, an impressive hotel overlooking the seaward end of nearby Bude golf course, amidst sheltered gardens with a welcoming southerly aspect. Close to town and just a short walk from the beach, it still manages to be quiet and private. In the same family for 39 years, the atmosphere is friendly and the service attentive.

Maer Lodge Hotel

The 18 well-appointed en suite bedrooms are tastefully decorated and feature all the amenities you would expect from a hotel with the fine reputation enjoyed by Maer Lodge. This attractive establishment makes an ideal base for exploring the region, in particular the North Cornish gems of Port Isaac, Tintagel, Boscastle, Clovelly and Hartland Point, just short drives away. It is also ideally placed for excellent cliffside walks, the sea, sandy beaches, scenic countryside vistas and the delights of the six nearby golf courses. The residents' bar serves refreshments at most times of the day, while the main lounge overlooks the lovely, sunny lawns - the perfect place to relax. Open all year. *Maer Lodge Hotel, Crooklets Beach, Bude, Cornwall EX23 8NG Tel: 01288 353306.*

Around Bude

Stratton — *Map 2 ref N2*

1½ miles E of Bude off the A39

Stratton is believed to have been founded by the ancient Romans. Its steeply sloping main street is lined with fine Georgian houses and cottages, many of them thatched. Its early-14th century parish church contains a Norman font and some striking early memorials and monumental brasses.

During the English Civil War, the ***Tree Inn*** was used as a centre of operations by the Royalist general, Sir Bevil Grenville, before he led his troops to victory at nearby ***Stamford Hill*** in May, 1643. The Iron Age earthwork which had been held by the Parliamentarians can be seen a mile away to the northwest. After the battle, the dead from both sides were buried in unmarked graves in Stratton churchyard. The Tree Inn was also the birthplace of the legendary Anthony Payne, a 7 foot giant who fought for the Royalist cause and was offered a post in Sir Bevil's household as a reward.

Cann Orchard bed and breakfast is a lovely listed farmhouse, mentioned in the Domesday Book. Situated down a quiet country

Cann Orchard

lane between Stratton and the pretty village of Marhamchurch, and just one and a half miles from Bude and the rugged beauty of the North Cornish coast, this warm and welcoming B&B has three very comfortable oak-beamed guest bedrooms, lovingly restored and attractively furnished. Set in three acres of lovely gardens and orchards, the farmhouse is stituated along the route taken by the Royalists to the Battle of Stamford Hill - a re-enactment is staged in Stratton every May by the Sealed Knot Society. An ideal centre for walkers, there are also excellent golf courses as well as surfing, sea fishing and horse-riding available within a two mile radius. Jonathan and Joanne Crocker make every guest feel most welcome in their handsome home. *Cann Orchard, Howard Lane, Stratton, Bude, Cornwall EX23 9TD Tel: 01288 352098.*

Launcells *Map 2 ref O2*

2 miles E of Bude off the A3072

Those with a liking for country churches should make a point of visiting this picturesque village. Set in a delightful wooded combe, ***St Swithin's*** is a medieval treasure which managed to escape the ravages of Victorian restorers. The surprisingly light and pleasant interior contains one of the finest sets of early bench ends in Cornwall - over 60 in all - each carved with a scene or symbol from the New Testament. Other noteworthy features are a Norman font which is finished in characteristic cable carving, a Tudor mural which, sadly, is now losing its colour, and a collection of early Barnstaple tiles which can be seen on the floor of the chancel.

In the churchyard can be seen the grave of the 19th century physician, scientist and inventor Sir Goldsworthy Gurney, the steam pioneer and builder of the castle at the mouth of the Bude canal. A bridge over the nearby stream leads to a holy well, one of over a hundred in the county which have become associated with pre-Norman saints, but whose origins often date back to pagan times.

Kilkhampton *Map 2 ref O1*

4 miles NE of Bude off the A39

A remarkable set of 16th century carved bench ends can be seen in Kilkhampton's part-12th century church. Although more numerous than at Launcells (there are more than 150), their craftsmanship is perhaps not as impressive. The church also contains several monuments to the Grenville family, a baroque organ which is said to have come from Westminster Abbey, and an ornately carved Norman doorway which is among the finest in the West Country.

Morwenstow *Map 2 ref N1*

5 miles N of Bude off the A39

This tiny settlement, whose agricultural income has in the distant past been supplemented by ill-gotten gains from the sea, is a good access point to the dramatic stretch of coastline known as the ***Hartland Peninsula***, with its wild jagged cliffs.

Morwenstow's part-Norman church has some impressive wagon roofs, a richly carved Norman font, and a medieval wall-painting of St Morwenna, the Celtic saint to whom the building is dedicated.

The village's most renowned former inhabitant is the eccentric vicar and poet, Robert Stephen Hawker, who arrived in 1834 and remained amongst his congregation of *'smugglers, wreckers and dissenters'* until his death in 1875. A colourful figure dressed in a purple cloak and long fisherman's boots, Hawker would spend much of his time striding across the clifftops, or writing verse and smoking (some accounts say opium) in a tiny driftwood hut he built for himself on the cliff. He was among the first to show concern about the number of merchant vessels which were coming to grief on this perilous stretch of coastline. Prior to his interventions, it was common for local criminals to use lights to lure unsuspecting ships onto the rocks. Hawker would often climb down to rescue shipwrecked crews from shore, or to carry back the bodies of drowned mariners so they could be given a Christian burial. A distinctive ships' figurehead in the churchyard marks the final resting place of the crew of the Caledonia, which went down in 1842.

At his own expense, Hawker built Morwenstow rectory to his own design, with chimneys representing the towers of various churches, Oxford colleges and, in the case of the broad kitchen chimney, his mother's gravestone. He is also remembered for reintroducing the annual harvest thanksgiving festival, a custom which now takes place all over the world. Some of Hawker's less worthy exploits included expelling his cat from the church for daring to catch a mouse on a Sunday, and playing a practical joke by sitting on a rock by the sea dressed as a mermaid (and singing as well!). His most famous poem is the rousing Cornish anthem, The Song of Western Men, which includes the stirring lines:

'And shall Trelawny die?
Here's the twenty-thousand Cornish men
Will know the reason why!'

Trewint — *Map 3 ref N3*

5 miles S of Bude off the A39

John Wesley often stayed here in this handsome village. His hosts' cottage, with its specially constructed prophets' room and pilgrims' garden, has been restored and is open to the public.

St Gennys — *Map 2 ref N3*

7 miles SW of Bude off the A39

This tiny isolated hamlet (pronounced with a hard 'g') lies in a spectacular hilltop position. Its tiny part-Norman church is dedicated to St Genesius, a martyr who is reputed to have picked up his head after an executioner had chopped it off, and holds a rare altar tabernacle.

Crackington Haven — *Map 2 ref M3*

7½ miles SW of Bude off the A39

A narrow undulating road runs along the coast past ***Widemouth Bay***, a striking expanse of sand open to the elements. These lanes wind their way back to the shoreline at Crackington Haven, one of the most dramatic spots on this formidable stretch of coast. This small and narrow sandy cove is approached down a steep-sided wooded combe which has a few houses, an inn and village shop at the bottom.

The beach itself is overlooked by sheer 400 foot high cliffs and jagged rocks, making it Cornwall's highest coastal point. It is difficult to imagine that sizable vessels once landed at this unwelcoming harbour to deliver their cargoes of limestone and Welsh coal and to collect loads of locally-quarried slate. The cliffs on either side are composed of extravagantly folded strata of volcanic rock which have given their name to a geological formation known as the ***Crackington Measures***. Although impressive to look at, the rock can often be loosely packed and the cliff edges should be approached with extreme caution.

Trenance is Cornish for *'place of the valley'*, and this handsome guest house was built halfway up a valley by a local builder, originally for his own family, in a designated Area of Outstanding Natural Beauty, on land owned by the National Trust and offering marvellous sea views. The nearby coastal path makes for excellent walks, and there are tennis courts and a safe sandy beach, as well as shops for essentials, close by. Historic Tintagel is a short drive away, as are the picturesque villages of Boscastle, Port Isaac and Clovelly. Among the many activities on offer in the area are golf, fishing,

Trenance Guest House

cycling and water skiing. Owners David and Jo Beldham offer guests a warm and friendly welcome. All round the house are a selection of watercolours by local artist Isabel Orr. The five tastefully decorated bedrooms are cosy, comfortable and charming; one has a four-poster bed, and all enjoy superb views. Full English breakfast or alternative. Evening meals, packed lunches and cream teas are also available on request. *Trenance Guest House, Crackington Haven, Nr Bude, Cornwall EX23 0JQ Tel: 01840 230273.*

There is some stunning clifftop walking to the south of Crackington Haven, particularly above the sandy cove known as ***The Strangles***. A few hundred yards further on, the footpath rises to over 700 feet at ***High Cliff***, one of the highest sea cliffs in Cornwall. Parts of the surrounding coastline were donated to the National Trust in memory of the RAF pilots who died in the Second World War.

Boscastle *Map 2 ref M4*

12 miles SW of Bude off the B3263

Lying on a delightful, unspoilt stretch of the north Cornwall coastline, this was a thriving seaport up to the 19th century and is now used by local inshore fishermen and visitors. The National Trust own and protect the harbour area as well as a considerable amount of the land and coastline in north Corwall. This ancient and picturesque fishing community stands in a combe at the head of a remarkable S-shaped inlet from the Atlantic.

The village grew up around, and takes its name from, the now demolished Bottreaux castle which was built by the de Botterell family in Norman times. Its unique natural harbour was formed by the rivers Valency and Jordan having to carve their way through a high slate cliff to the sea.

The Old Coach House is an impressive rural bed and breakfast located here in this quiet countryside village, just three miles from historic Tintagel. This 300 year-old former coach store and stables, altered to make a house about 100 years ago, has a relaxed, friendly feel about it and attracts visitors from all over the world. Very near the sea with some excellent walking along the coastal path, this handsome stonework establishment has eight charming rooms, all en suite. Three of these are family rooms; the two ground-

The Old Coach House

floor rooms are fully equipped with amenities for people with disabilities. Each room is tastefully fitted out with pine furnishings, and overlooks nearby farmland. Breakfast is served in the large conservatory attached to the back of the house, which offers views of the church and Forrabury Common. Smoked fish with scrambled egg, full English or Continental breakfast are among the choices offered to guests. There are a number of fine pubs and restaurants nearby for evening meals. AA (3Q); RAC listed; Two crowns from the English Tourist Board. *The Old Coach House, Tintagel Road, Boscastle, Cornwall PL35 0AS Tel: 01840 250398.*

Boscastle harbour's inner jetty was built by the renowned Elizabethan seafarer, Sir Richard Grenville, when the village was prospering as a fishing, grain and slate port. The outer jetty was added 350 years later when Boscastle was being developed as a seaport for the manganese and iron ore mines near Launceston. This latter structure was accidentally blown up by a stray mine during the Second World War, and had to be repaired by the National Trust at considerable expense.

The Trust owns the harbour and much of the coastline around Boscastle. The spectacular slate headlands on either side of the community provide some excellent - if demanding - walking. The village itself is set around a steep broad thoroughfare lined with attractive houses, inns and shops, most of which cater for the holiday-maker. A tourist information centre is located in the old forge by the harbour; there is also an interesting ***Witchcraft Museum*** which contains some sinister relics of the ancient black arts. The esteemed author Thomas Hardy was a regular visitor to Boscastle when he worked as an architect on the restoration of the church at St Juliot, two miles southeast. The village appears as *'Castle Boterel'* in Hardy's early novel, *A Pair of Blue Eyes*. Other attractions in the village include the ***Cave Holography & Illusion Exhibition***, and ***Lye Rock***, a great place for puffin-spotting.

St Juliot, Near Boscastle — *Map 2 ref M4*

12 miles SW of Bude off the B3263

Hardy's church at St Juliot is a gem of a hidden place (Hardy called the hamlet *'Endelstow'* in his novel). It lies in the wooded valley of the fast-flowing river Valency and can be reached from Boscastle along a lovely footpath, or by road via the B3263.

It was here in 1870 that Hardy met his wife-to-be, Emma Gifford, the rector's sister-in-law. (She later professed that the young architect had already appeared to her in a dream, and wrote how she was *'immediately arrested by his familiar appearance'*.) Much of the couple's courtship took place along the wild stretch of coastline between Boscastle and Crackington Haven, and when Emma died over 40 years later, Hardy returned to St Juliot to erect a memorial to her in the church. (A similar memorial was erected to the writer following his death in 1928.)

Two miles further southwest, the B3263 crosses the mile-long ***Rocky Valley***, a curious rock-strewn cleft in the landscape which has a character all of its own. In the wooded upper reaches can be found the impressive 40 foot waterfall known as ***St Nectan's Kieve***. St Nectan was a Celtic hermit whose cell is believed to have stood beside the basin, or kieve, at the foot of the cascade, and whose grave is said to lie beneath it. As the valley winds northwards, it gradually becomes deeper and more gorge-like until, at its end, it suddenly opens out, depositing the river directly into the sea.

Tintagel

The romantic remains of ***Tintagel Castle*** stand on top of ***Tintagel Head***. Prior to a series of rock falls in the 19th century, this formidable headland was connected to the mainland by a natural stone bridge; now only a narrow isthmus remains. Many like to believe

Tintagel Castle

that this was the birthplace of the legendary King Arthur, or even that it was the site of Camelot, the mythical headquarters of the Knights of the Round Table (other possibilities are Caerleon in Wales and South Cadbury in Somerset). Fragments of a Celtic monastic house dating from the 6th century have been uncovered on the headland; their origins coincide with the activities of the Welsh military leader on which the Arthurian legends are thought to be based; however, the fortification we see today was founded by Reginald Earl of Cornwall, the illegitimate son of Henry I, in the 12th century, over 600 years after Arthur would have died. Whatever the true heritage of Tintagel castle, the scramble down towards the sea and back up to its clifftop site 250 feet above the Atlantic is a breathtaking experience.

Tintagel, of course, owes much of its popularity to the Arthurian connection. One of its most noteworthy attractions is ***'King Arthur's Halls'***; these were built in the 1930's by devotees of the legends and include the ***'Hall of Chivalry'***, a room with over 70 stained-glass windows depicting the coats of arms of the Knights of the Round Table. Elsewhere, Arthurian eating places and souvenir shops abound.

The Cornishman Inn is an atmospheric public house and bed and breakfast in the heart of King Arthur country in Tintagel, within easy walking distance of superb views along the cliffs and Tintagel Castle itself. The pub serves up fine ales and wines, and has an extensive bar menu. Drinks and food can be enjoyed in front of the roaring fires in winter, or out on the handsome flowered terrace when the weather is fine. The 10 en suite rooms are comfortable and quiet. Proprietors Jeremy and Rochelle are friendly, welcoming hosts who make every effort to ensure their guests have a relaxing

The Cornishman Inn

and memorable stay. The Cornishman's village countryside location is secluded and restful, while still in close proximity to the sea, historical places of interest, shops and other amenities. There is a range of recreational facilities within the area, including four championship golf courses only a short drive away. There are also a number of hidden beaches and coves in the area, including Trebarwith Strand and the Bossiney Cove nearby, with their golden sands and magnificent scenery. *The Cornishman Inn, Tintagel, Cornwall PL34 0DB Tel: 01840 770238 Fax: 01840 770078 email: cmaninn@aol.com*

The ***Parish Church*** is set some distance away from the centre of the village on an exposed cliff. Norman in origin, it retains substantial fragments of its original fabric, including the font, windows and sections of the walls. There is also a good early 15th century monumental brass and a rare Roman tinners' milestone from the 4th century AD - one of only five surviving examples in Cornwall.

Perhaps the finest building in Tintagel is the ***Old Post Office***, a small 14th century slate-built manor house which in the 19th century found new life as a letter-receiving station. Now owned by the National Trust, this charming and strangely organic-looking structure has been carefully restored to its Victorian livery.

A good sandy beach can be found a couple of miles to the south of Tintagel at ***Trebarwith Strand***, one of the few breaks in the wild craggy cliffscape.

Around Tintagel

Delabole

Map 2 ref M5

2 miles S of Tintagel off the B3314

Delabole, slightly inland of Trebarwith, is the location of the most famous ***slate quarry*** in Cornwall. High-quality dark blue slate has been quarried here without interruption since Tudor times, and this prolonged activity has resulted in an open cavity some 500 feet deep and a mile and a half in circumference - the deepest manmade hole in Britain. At one time, most of the buildings in the county incorporated roofing slates or flagstones from Delabole, and over 500 people were employed blasting and slicing the stone into attractively named standard sizes: *'Ladies'*, *'Countesses'*, *'Duchesses'*, *'Queens'* and *'Imperials'*. Although the introduction of less expensive substitutes has caused a steady decline in the industry, the traditional demand from builders and monumental stonemasons has been supplemented by a demand for powdered slate from the paint and cosmetics industries. The operators have built a viewing platform which offers a breathtaking panorama of the quarry workings; there is also a visitors' centre which incorporates a slate museum and a showroom.

Once known as *'the great slate road'*, the lanes to the west of Delabole used to carry vast quantities of stone to the harbours at Port Gaverne, Port Isaac and Port Quin (some slate was also exported through Boscastle).

St Teath — *Map 2 ref L5*

5 miles S of Tintagel off the A39

Trehannick Farm is an airy and spacious 17th century house offering bed and breakfast accommodation. Set in 180 lush acres, the three guest bedrooms afford marvellous views across the rolling countryside near Bodmin. Decorated throughout in classic florals and in a style befitting the farm's 17th century origins (including, in the family room, a wonderful four-poster bed), this welcoming establishment occupies a prime position near to several wonderful

Trehannick Farm

local walks and historic sites along the coast nearby. Guests take their meals - an excellent range of breakfasts are available - in the charming dining room. Adorned with lovely furniture and handsome antiques throughout, this distinguished B&B attracts visitors from all over the world, including the US, Australia, New Zealand, and from elsewhere in Europe.

Mrs Jenny Bass and her friendly, efficient staff assure visitors a very warm welcome and the best in personal service and a relaxed atmosphere, making any stay here a true delight. *Trehannick Farm, St Teath, Bodmin, Cornwall PL30 3JW Tel: 01208 850312*

Port Isaac *Map 2 ref L5*

5 miles SW of Tintagel off the B3314

This lovely old fishing community of stone and slate houses is divided by narrow alleyways, or *drangs* (one goes by the charming name of *'Squeeze-Belly Alley'*), and has a lovely small beach.

At one time, huge quantities of herring were landed here. After the arrival of the railway, these were gutted and packed in the village's many fish cellars before being despatched by train to Britain's inland centres of population by train. One of these old cellars is now an inshore lifeboat station, while others are used at boathouses or retail outlets.

Port Gaverne Hotel is a picturesque whitewashed establishment occupying an enviable position, sheltered on a spectacular small cove just half a mile from the 1,000 year-old fishing village of Port Isaac. This early 17th century coastal inn with 17 comfortable bedrooms offers good accommodation, food, drink and cheerful attention to its guests. In addition there are six self-catering cottages opposite the hotel, and two large flats overlooking the cove - Upper Tregudda, consisting of a large lounge, dining room, utility room (washing machine/tumble drier), kitchen (dishwasher/microwave), two bathrooms and four bedrooms. Lower Tregudda occupies the ground floor, and features a sea-facing kitchen/dining room (dishwasher and microwave), lounge, utility room (washing machine and tumble drier), shower room, four bedrooms and two bathrooms.

Port Gaverne Hotel

In Midge's Restaurant, residents and non-residents alike can enjoy superb fresh garden produce, local beef and lamb, fish, lobster and crab in season. All this and within easy distance of lovely walks, sheltered swimming, golf, fishing, riding, surfing and sailing make Port Gaverne a welcoming and ideally-situated haven of peace and comfort. *The Port Gaverne Hotel and Midge's Restaurant, Near Port Isaac, Cornwall PL29 3SQ Tel: 01208 880244 Freephone: 500 657867 Fax: 01208 880151.*

St Endellion — *Map 2 ref L6*

5 miles SW of Tintagel off the B3314

This charming village has a church built of Lundy island granite and dedicated to St Endelienta, a Celtic saint who lived solely, so they say, on milk - and who passed away after her trusty cow was killed in a dispute with a farmer. The village also hosts a twice-yearly music festival. Nearby, ***Long Cross Victorian Gardens*** offer a chance to visit a peaceful and attractive haven resplendent with 19th century plants and plantings.

Port Quin — *Map 2 ref K5*

7 miles SW of Tintagel off the B3314

This picturesque coastal hamlet is overlooked by a Regency faux-Gothic folly on ***Doyden's Point***. When Portquin's slate trade was ended by the coming of the railways, it went through such a severe period of decline that at one time outsiders thought that the entire population had been washed away in a great storm. The village remained deserted for decades, but was eventually purchased and restored by the National Trust. Today it is a seasonal community with a very pleasant atmosphere which is arranged around a clutch of National Trust-owned holiday cottages. The offshore rock formations are known as the Cow and Calf.

Just west of Portquin, the small peninsula of land to the north and east of the Camel Estuary is a lovely stretch of country which is entirely free of through traffic. The table-topped ***Pentire Head***, to the extreme northwest, offers some excellent walking with magnificent views over the Camel Estuary. The northernmost tip, ***the Rump***, is a promontory of hard greenstone which has been eroded into a series of extraordinary pinnacles; this was the site of an Iron Age hill fort, one of three on the headland. The area is known for its wild tamarisk, an elegant flowering shrub more commonly found around the shores of the Mediterranean. Pentire Head was saved from commercial development in the 1930s after local campaigners raised enough funds to purchase the land and donate it to the National Trust.

Polzeath and New Polzeath

Map 2 ref K6

10 miles SW of Tintagel off the B3314

The small resort of Polzeath has a broad west-facing beach which is popular with surfers. With its fine sand, caves and tidal rock pools, it is also a superb location for families with young children. Former Poet Laureate John Betjeman extols Polzeath in much of his verse.

Set amid spectacular scenery just a short walk from fine beaches and the coastal path, ***The Cornish Cottage Hotel & Gourmet Restaurant*** is a handsome and impressive establishment offering beautifully appointed en suite bedrooms, some furnished in a traditional country cottage style. Situated in a sheltered and peaceful position overlooking New Polzeath, the atmosphere in this homely and comfortable hotel is tranquil and relaxed. The Cornish Cottage has a heated outdoor swimming pool, open from May to October.

The Cornish Cottage Hotel & Restaurant

The hotel also boasts a magnificent handcrafted Italian-designed bar and guests' sun lounge. Superb walking, golfing, fishing, sailing and surfing are all well catered for in the area; many National Trust properties and gardens are also within easy distance. The restaurant boasts a superb menu of fresh local produce and locally landed fish and seafood; under the aegis of innovative chef Martin Walker it offers a range of imaginative and tempting dishes. Holder of 2 AA Rosettes for fine cuisine; noted in the Good Food Guide, Trenchermans, and Food in Cornwall . *The Cornish Cottage Hotel & Gourmet Restaurant, Bishops Hill, New Polzeath, Near Rock, Cornwall PL27 6UF Tel: 01208 862213 Fax: 01208 862259.*

Brea Hill, Near Trebetherick

Map 2 ref K6

10 miles SW of Tintagel off the B3314

Brea Hill looks out over the submerged sandbank known as the ***Doom Bar***, a hidden hazard which has spelled the end for many a vessel seeking shelter from Atlantic storms.

Standing in an exquisite position on the inland side of the hill, the delightful ***church of St Enodoc*** is a largely Norman structure with a squat 13th century stone spire. On a number of occasions throughout its history, windblown sand has almost completely buried the little building, and at such times entry could only be gained through an opening in the roof. The sand was finally cleared away in the 1860's, when the church was restored. The bell in the tower came from an Italian ship which was wrecked nearby in 1875.

St Enodoc's beautiful churchyard contains many graves of shipwrecked mariners who came to grief on this treacherous stretch of coastline. The remains of Sir John Betjeman and his mother lie here too. The fondly remembered Poet Laureate spend most of his childhood holidays in the villages and coves which border the Camel Estuary. He has a lasting affection for the local people, and they and the surrounding landscape provided the inspiration for many of his poems, among them Sunday Afternoon Service at St Enodoc's. The churchyard stands beside St Enodoc Golf Course, a natural golf links which is regarded as one of the most scenic in the country.

Close by and situated in almost two acres of beautiful and secluded gardens, ***Bodare Hotel*** is an extensive, impressive country house hotel only yards from ***Daymer Beach***, which provides some of the safest sea bathing in Cornwall. This attractive, family-run hotel is also only three minutes' walk from St Enodoc Golf Course. Surfing, sailing, riding and water ski-ing facilities are also all close at hand. The Bodare Hotel has two comfortable and well-appointed lounges, a cosy, well-stocked bar and a handsome dining room over-

Bodare Hotel

looking the magnificent gardens. The meals and wines on offer are superb, as is the service. The supremely comfortable guest bedrooms are all en suite. Jason Carrodus manages to make every guest feel special at this warm and welcoming family-run hotel; the bywords here are care, conscientiousness and efficiency. A stay in this attractive, peaceful and gracious setting will certainly be a memorable and very pleasant and relaxing one. *Bodare Hotel, Daymer Bay, Nr Wadebridge, Cornwall PL27 6SA Tel: 01208 863210 Fax: 01208 863220.*

Hallworthy — *Map 3 ref N4*

8 miles E of Tintagel off the A395

The handsome and impressive whitewashed ***Wilsey Down Hotel*** in Hallworthy, just five miles northeast of Camelford, offers superior accommodation. The six charming and tasteful rooms (two en suite - for the more daring guest, legend has it that room 9 is haunted!) meet a high standard of comfort. In the welcoming, large

Wilsey Down Hotel

and airy public bar, the handsome stone fireplaces and pine panelling add to the warm and cosy atmosphere. The unusually extensive range of tempting bar meals can be enjoyed here or in the beer garden. Cream teas are served throughout the summer. The restaurant is quiet and intimate, with a menu noteworthy for its variety and excellence - main courses include steaks, chicken, pork, fish and vegetarian dishes, all home-cooked using local ingredients where available. Located near the north Cornwall coast, sea-side or countryside walks, historic Boscastle and Tintagel and Bodmin Moor, this lovely establishment is run with care by co-proprietors Jane Brendon and Sharman Tucker, farmers' wives who are thoroughly enjoying their venture into catering and hostelry. Their enthusiasm shows in the thoroughness and commitment they bring to the personal service and warm welcome they give their guests. *The Wilsey Down Hotel, Hallworthy, Camelford, Cornwall PL32 9SH Tel: 01840 261205.*

Camelford — *Map 2 ref M5*

5 miles SE of Tintagel off the A39

This small former wool town contains an interesting museum of rural life, the ***North Cornwall Museum*** and ***Art Gallery***, housed in a converted coach house, and the ***Museum of Historic Cycling***. Its ***Crowdy Reservoir*** makes an excellent spot for trout fishing.

CHAPTER TWO
Southeast Cornwall

Polperro's Harbour Entrance

Chapter 2 - Area Covered

For precise location of places please refer to the colour maps found at the rear of the book.

2
Southeast Cornwall

Introduction

The River Tamar forms a boundary with Devon right down to the river's estuary on the south coast. Where the north is dominated by high cliffs, the south is a series of secluded rocky coves and bays. Here, places such as Liskeard, in the valley of the East Looe and Seaton rivers, East and West Looe, Torpoint, along the Tamar Estuary, Lostwithiel, along the Fowey Estuary, and innumerable cloistered and scenic villages and small seaside towns are redolent with the legacy of their long history as fishing, privateering and smuggling centres. The inescapable romance of the landscape, which has inspired writers, artists, natives and visitors for centuries, is complemented by gentle Gulf Stream breezes, assuring mild weather throughout spring, summer and autumn. This part of Cornwall is renowned for its characterful resorts, miles of beaches, bustling quaysides and busy market towns.

Liskeard

Standing on an undulating site between the valleys of the East Looe and Seaton rivers, Liskeard is a pleasant old market town which was one of Cornwall's five medieval Stannary towns (the others being Bodmin, Lostwithiel, Truro and Helston). The name comes from the Latin word for tin, *stannum*, and these five towns were the only ones licensed to weigh and stamp the metal. The town has a long history as a centre for mineral extraction: for centuries, the medieval Cornish tinners brought their smelted tin down from Bodmin

Moor for weighing, stamping and taxing, then in the early 19th century, great quantities of copper ore from the nearby ***Caradon mines*** and granite from the ***Cheesewring quarries*** were loaded onto barges here and despatched to the coast along the newly-constructed Looe canal. In the 1850's, the canal was replaced by the Looe valley branch of the Great Western Railway, a scenic stretch of line which still operates today although its industrial cargoes have long been replaced by passenger holiday traffic.

Thankfully now bypassed by the busy A38 Plymouth to Bodmin road, Liskeard's narrow streets contain a number of interesting old buildings, including the curious ***Italianate Guildhall*** and ***Stuart House***, a handsome Jacobean residence in which Charles I is believed to have stayed for a week during the English Civil War. The surprisingly large parish church, one of the most substantial in Cornwall, reflects the town's former importance as a centre for agriculture and mineral extraction, and there are also a number of elegant Georgian houses and coaching inns. Perhaps Liskeard's most unusual feature can be found in Well Lane, where an arched grotto marks the site of ***Pipe Well***, a medieval spring which is reputed to have curative powers.

Crows Nest Inn is a very attractive country public house set in the quiet and scenic village of Darite, just a few miles north of Liskeard. This handsome establishment offers a range of delicious bar snacks, as well as a full menu for evening meals and traditional Sunday roast. All the food is home-cooked and home-prepared. The bar is extensively stocked; St Austell beers are among the liquid

The Crows Nest Inn

refreshment on offer, to be enjoyed in front of the roaring open log fire or, in warmer weather, outside in the lovely beer garden, which has its own working well. The decor in this welcoming pub is traditional, with an extensive collection of horse bits, old forge bellows, beamed ceilings and exposed stonework walls. Friendly landlords Sue and Roy Hughes are happy to make up sandwiches and fill flasks for picnickers, and guarantee all visitors are hearty welcome. *Crows Nest Inn, Darite, Liskeard, Cornwall PL14 5JQ Tel: 01579 345930.*

Around Liskeard

Dobwalls — *Map 3 ref N7*

3 miles W of Liskeard off the A38

The popular ***Dobwalls Adventure Park*** and ***Mr Thorburn's Edwardian Countryside*** can be found on the northern edge of the village from which it takes its name. The park contains a number of contrasting attractions, including the Forest Railway, a two mile long miniature steam railway whose locomotives and rolling stock are based on the old North American railroad. There is also an indoor railway museum and an extensive adventure playground. The charming Edwardian countryside museum features a permanent exhibition on the life and work of the English wildlife artist, Archibald Thorburn. On site there is also an art gallery and ***Cornish Craft Centre***.

The famous ***Carnglaze Slate Caverns*** lie two miles west in the lovely wooded valley of the River Loveny, a mile to the north on the A38. Slate for use in the building trade was first quarried in these vast man-made caverns in the 14th century. The largest chamber is over 300 foot high and was once used by smugglers as a secret rum store. The lichen on the cavern walls is covered with minute droplets of water which reflect the available light in the most magical way. Visitors can see the remains of the tramway which was built to haul the stone to the surface from the lower levels, and at the deepest level there is a subterranean pool which is filled with the clearest blue-green water.

The Highwayman is a distinguished public house situated in this charming village location at the edge of Bodmin Moor, two miles from Golitha Falls, where the Beast of Bodmin has been sighted. Just one mile from Dobwalls Theme Park and from Trago Mills, this stone-built 18th century former farmhouse was converted to a pub in 1962. A large painting of a highwayman graces the back ex-

The Highwayman

terior wall of the pub. The interior boasts exposed timbers on walls and ceilings, large inglenook fireplace, a handsome wood-panelled bar, coaching lights on the wall and a wall-mounted case containing original flintlocks and pistols dating back to the 1770's. There are glazed leaded windows above the bar; the range of naval plaques on the beams reflect the pub's popularity with local naval families. There are real ales on offer in addition to hearty bar meals and other refreshments. Owners Sue and Stewart West offer one of the warmest welcomes you'll come across anywhere in Cornwall, and are anxious to ensure that every visitor is made to feel at home. *The Highwayman, Dobwalls, Liskeard, Cornwall PL14 6JD Tel: 01579 320114.*

St Cleer

Map 3 ref O7

2 miles N of Liskeard off the B3254

This sizable village lies in the heart of bleak former mining country on the southern fringe of Bodmin Moor. The settlement is arranged around the parish church, a largely 15th century building with a striking granite tower and a Norman doorway which has survived from an earlier building. To the northeast of the churchyard, another 15th century granite structure marks the site of a holy well whose waters are reputed to have restorative powers. Visitors to such holy wells commonly leave a personal item such as a handkerchief behind them - these can sometimes be seen hanging from nearby branches. Half a mile east of the village centre stands ***Trethevy Quoit***, a massive enclosed Neolithic chamber which originally formed the core of a vast earthwork mound. The largest structure of its type in Cornwall, it is believed to be around 5,000 years old and has much in common with those found in west Penwith. On the opposite (western) side of the village, the ***Doniert Stone*** is a tall stone cross which was erected as a memorial to King Durngarth, a Cornish king who is thought to have drowned in the nearby River Fowey around 870 AD. Sadly now broken into two pieces, it is carved with a Latin inscription which, translated, reads *'Erected for Doniert for the good of his soul.'* A little further west, the River Fowey descends for half a mile through dense broad-leaved woodland in a delightful series of cascades known as ***Golitha Falls***, as well as the delightful ***Siblyback Lake***.

The 300 year-old ***Stag Inn*** is located in the lovely and historic village of St Cleer. Decorated in traditional country pub style, with exposed timber ceilings, open fires, exposed stonework, wood-panelled bar and collection of horse brasses, handsome trophy cabinet and striking old photographs and hunting images adorning the walls, this welcoming establishment serves up very good real ales in a friendly and cosy atmosphere. In the restaurant, pew-style seating and in the bar large barrel tables enhance the traditional ambience. Three menus are available to hungry diners: one for tasty lunchtime/bar meals, one for full evening meals, and a specials board featuring that day's particular offers. A must for the real ale enthusiast, The Stag features 40 guest ales a year, in addition to its normal

The Stag Inn

extensive stock of satisfying beers, wines and spirits. *The Stag Inn, Fore Street, St Cleer, Liskeard, Cornwall PL14 5DA Tel: 01579 342305.*

St Keyne — *Map 3 ref O8*

2½ miles S of Liskeard off the B3254

This small village is home to the fascinating ***Paul Corin's Mechanical Music Centre***, a unique museum of mechanical instruments housed in a lovely old mill which stands near the bridge over the East Looe River, half a mile east of the centre of the village. Exhibits include street, cafe and fairground organs, all of which are kept in working order and played on a regular basis.

One of the more unusual episodes in St Keyne's history took place during the reign of the Catholic Mary Tudor, when the local rector and his wife (who had married during the reign of the Protestant Edward VI) were dragged from their bed in the middle of the night and placed on the village stocks.

Another famous holy well, known as ***St Keyne Well***, lies a mile south of the village beneath a great tree which is said to bear the leaves of four different species. According to local legend, the first member of a newly-married couple to drink from the spring will be the one who wears the trousers, a notion which captured the imagination of Victorian newlyweds and brought them here in their thousands.

Duloe — *Map 3 ref N8*

4 miles S of Liskeard off the B3254

This charming village is the location of a circle of eight standing quartz stones, 38 feet in diameter, reputedly older than Stonehenge. In addition the ***Church of St Cuby and St Leonard*** has a 13th century tower.

Looe

At the mouth of the East and West Looe rivers stands the bustling coastal resort and fishing port of Looe. Originally two separate towns facing each other across the estuary, ***East*** and ***West Looe*** were first connected by a bridge in the early 15th century, and were officially incorporated in 1883. The present seven-arched bridge dates from the 19th century and is wide enough to carry the A387 Polperro road.

In common with many other Cornish coastal settlements which have had to scratch a living by whatever means available, Looe has always been something of a jack-of-all-trades. As well as having a long-established pilchard fishing fleet, it has also served the mineral extractors of Bodmin Moor as a port for exporting tin - and later, copper - ore.

As early as 1800, a bathing machine was constructed at the top of Looe's sandy beach, and when visitors began to arrive in numbers with the coming of the railway in 1859, the town began to develop as a resort. More recently, Looe has established itself as Britain's premier shark-fishing centre, regularly hosting an International Sea Angling Festival.

Trelaske Country Hotel and Restaurant is the ideal location for a holiday in the country, whilst being only three-quarters of a mile from the beach and two miles equidistant from the historic fishing villages of Looe and Polperro. Its four acres of magnificent lawns and gardens are quite delightful, with an abundance of plants and shrubs surrounded by established trees and hedges. The hotel is personally owned and managed by Mr and Mrs Rawlings, who are always available to ensure that their high standards of personal service and comfort are maintained at all times.

Each of the seven bedrooms is individually appointed, revealing meticulous care for detail and luxury touches. Full English breakfast is served in the restaurant; Continental breakfast can be served in your room if preferred. The restaurant is certainly one of the best in the area, drawing its produce from all over the world: the finest salmon from Scotland, and other fresh fish from one of the best European fish markets - at Looe, right on the doorstep. The restaurant is open to non-residents and maintains consistently high

Trelaske Country Hotel and Restaurant

standards of food and wines. *Trelaske Country Hotel and Restaurant, Polperro Road, Looe, Cornwall PL13 2JS Tel: 01503 262159 Fax: 01503 265360.*

Over the years, Looe has evolved into a small seaside resort which has managed to retain a good deal of its original character, despite the annual invasion of holiday-makers. The old quarters on either side of the river are mazes of narrow lanes lined with old stone fisherman's cottages and inns, some of which are partially constructed from old ships' timbers. The 16th century ***Guildhall*** in East Looe is now an impressive local ***Museum***. The ***Living from the Sea Museum*** and ***Southeast Cornwall Discovery Centre*** also merit a visit.

In summer, pleasure boats depart from the quay for trips along the coast to Polperro and Fowey, and boat trips can also be taken to ***St George's Island*** half a mile offshore. Now a privately-run bird sanctuary, this was once the refuge of the notorious pirate and smuggler, Black Joan, who along with her brother Fyn terrorised the population of this lonely stretch of coast. The ***Looe Valley Line*** runs from Liskeard to Looe, taking in Coombe, St Keyne and many breathtaking local sights, with walks available from each station.

Cleese Farm bed and breakfast is a superior establishment with a large guests' sitting room and two spacious, light and airy guest bedrooms (one double, one family) handsomely decorated in country cottage style, each with its own fireplace. These south and west facing rooms afford superb views. This working dairy farm is located where the wooded Morval valley meets the Millendreath valley leading to the sea. There are peaceful walks through the nearby

Cleese Farm

woods, and the historic 15th century church at Morval attracts many interested visitors. The setting is quiet and secluded, while still being quite near the main roads to Plymouth and Looe and a range of sporting and leisure activities on offer in the surrounding area. Guests are assured a friendly, hospitable welcome; proprietor Janet Gill and her family make every effort to ensure that guests have a comfortable, relaxing and pleasant stay. The full English breakfasts are hearty and delicious. *Cleese Farm, Nomansland, Looe, Cornwall PL13 1PB Tel: 01503 240224.*

Around Looe

Pelynt — *Map 3 ref N9*

3 miles NW of Looe off the B3359

This charming village is well known for its quaint architecture (including the church, which has an unusual classical aisle dating from 1680), narrow streets and ***Banjo Pier***, and as a splendid setting for a relaxing and enjoyable holiday.

Talehay Farm is a charming, welcoming bed and breakfast with self-catering holiday cottages located only a few miles from Looe and Polperro, in countryside designated as an Area of Outstanding Natural Beauty. This quiet haven just three miles from the coast, a 17th century former working farmstead now converted to accommodate three guest bedrooms and four holiday cottages, makes a

Talehay Farm and Cottages

feature of the lush, established gardens in the grounds. Many of the farm's original features - exposed oak beams, slate window sills, open log fires - add a grace and charm enhanced by the antique furniture and tasteful, comfortable decor. The views across open countryside are superb. The delicious breakfasts make use of local produce, including eggs from the farm's own free-range hens, and such delights as home-made marmalade. Local amenities include golf, riding, fishing, boating, tennis and leisure complex. Talehay Farm makes for a convenient, comfortable base from which to explore Plymouth, Truro, the coast, the Lost Gardens of Heligan and many other historic and scenic sites. *Talehay Farm, Tremaine, Pelynt, Nr Looe, Cornwall PL13 2LT Tel: 01503 220252.*

Polperro *Map 3 ref N9*

3½ miles SW of Looe off the A387

This lovely old fishing community is many people's idea of the archetypal Cornish village. It stands at the point where a steep-sided wooded combe converges with a narrow tidal inlet from the sea. Its steep narrow streets and alleyways are piled high with white-painted fishermen's cottages, many of which have now been converted into art galleries and specialist shops.

Polperro Harbour

All routes seem to lead down to Polperro's highly photogenic double harbour, a working fishing port which normally contains an assortment of attractive inshore fishing vessels. The mouth of the inner harbour was fitted with movable timber gates after a southeasterly storm destroyed over 20 boats which were sheltering there in the early 19th century (they have now been replaced by a modern tidal floodgate).

Polperro has had a long association with smuggling: the practice was so rife in the 18th century that many of the village's inhabitants were involved in shipping, storing or transporting contraband goods. To combat the problem, H M Customs and Excise established the first *'preventive station'* in Cornwall here in the early 1800's. The atmosphere and events of those days are brought to life in a fascinating ***Smugglers' Museum*** which can be found near the inner harbour.

Another attraction is a model village of old Polperro, which is set within pleasant flower-filled gardens. Houses of interest include ***Couch's House*** (1595), ***House on Props***, and the ***Old Watch House***. A cliffpath leads to bays and beaches. Modern Polperro has had to succumb to the holiday industry - in summer, cars are banned from the narrow streets.

Murrayton — *Map 3 ref O9*

2 miles NE of Looe off the B3247

Here in a sheltered, wooded valley is the home of a famous ***Monkey Sanctuary*** - the world's first protected colony of Amazonian Woolly monkeys, established in 1964. It was set up to provide a stable setting for Woolly monkeys rescued from lives of isolation in zoos and as pets. The monkeys are allowed to roam freely and visitors are able to view them, along with a variety of other animals and birds, at close quarters. Regular talks and indoor displays explain more about monkey life and their natural habitat, the Amazonian Rainforest.

Seaton — *Map 3 ref O9*

3 miles E of Looe off the B3247

Seaton has an excellent sandy beach, once favoured as a landing place for smugglers. The coastal footpath to the west provides some fine clifftop walking.

Whitsand Bay — *Map 3 ref O9*

6 miles E of Looe off the B3247

The most impressive stretch of beach in southeast Cornwall is found along the shore here. More a series of coves than a continuous expanse of sand, the bay runs between Portwrinkle and Rame on the southwestern side of the Rame peninsula. To gain access to the beach, visitors should park in one of the car parks arranged at intervals along this highly scenic stretch of coast road, and then descend by way of a steep footpath. Lifeguards are on duty at busy times.

Torpoint

For those wishing to cross the Tamar Estuary (here called the *Hamoaze*) by car, a 24-hour vehicle ferry plies back and forth between Devonport and Torpoint. The latter stands on the northern arm of the Rame peninsula and is a small industrial boat-building and dormitory town which faces the naval dockyard across the Estuary.

The atmosphere is very different at ***Antony House***, a delightful National Trust-owned property which lies between the A374 and the estuary of the River Lynher, a mile and a half northwest. Considered one of the finest early Georgian country mansions in Cornwall, it was constructed between 1718 and 1729 of pale silver-grey stone brought in by sea from Pentewan, near Mevagissey.

The design is neoclassical in feel and consists of a forecourt enclosed by brick colonnades, with east and west wings fashioned in red brick. The interior is noted for its tapestries, panelling and fine 18th-century furniture, the most impressive of which can be seen in the dining room and library.

Around Torpoint

Millbrook *Map3 ref Q9*

2 miles S of Torpoint off the B3247

The Mark of Friendship public house is a friendly, comfortable establishment located down a quiet street amid scenic rural vistas and close to the sea, in the picturesque village of Millbrook, near Whitsand Bay. Popular with walkers, locals and visitors alike, this 300 year-old pub was formerly three separate cottages. The food on

The Mark of Friendship

offer is all good-quality home-cooked fare, using fresh local ingredients including fish and seafood. Once a month there are *'international'* evenings exploring the cuisine of far-off lands such as China, India, and Italy. Snacks and meals can be washed down with a selection of real ales and choice wines. Plans are also afoot to construct two en suite guest bedrooms, should you wish to prolong your stay in this delightful area. *The Mark of Friendship, 5 New Street, Millbrook, Cornwall PL10 1BY Tel: 01752 822253.*

Rame

Map 3 ref Q9

3 miles S of Torpoint off the B3247

Located at the southeastern end of Whitsand Bay, it's worth making a detour through Rame village to get to the spectacular ***Rame Head***. As the road enters the village, it curves around the 13th century ***Church of St Germanus***, a handsome structure with a tall west tower and spire which for centuries has served as a mariners' landmark. On the headland itself, visitors can park near the coastguards' station and walk over to the ruined 14th century chapel which is perched dramatically on top of a cone-shaped promontory. The ***Eddystone Lighthouse*** lies 10 miles offshore and can be seen on a clear day; the English fleet has their first encounter with the Spanish Armada to the southwest of here, in July 1588.

Cawsand and Kingsand

Map 3 ref Q9

3 miles S of Torpoint off the B3247

These adjoining communities are former fishing villages which owe much of their past prosperity to the smuggling industry. In the late 18th and early 19th centuries, thousands of barrels of brandy, silk and other contraband were landed here and carried through the narrow streets in the dead of night. For centuries, the small stream running into Cawsand Bay formed the county boundary between Saxon Devon and Celtic Cornwall, an administrative quirk which placed one half of the village in Cornwall (Cawsand) and the other in Devon (Kingsand).

Before the Plymouth Breakwater was completed in 1840, the Royal Navy fleet used to shelter from southwesterly gales by anchoring in Cawsand Bay, another factor which added to the prosperity of the place and left it with a surprising number of inns. There is an unusual end-on view of the breakwater from here and, to the east, there is some good easy coastal walking around the bay to ***Mount Edgcumbe House***, from where the Cremyll passenger ferry crosses to Plymouth.

St Germans

Map 3 ref P8

2 miles NW of Torpoint off the A374

St Germans gives little indication of its former prominence. For half a century before the Anglo-Saxon diocese of Cornwall was incorporated with Exeter in 1043, this quiet backwater was, in fact, a cathedral city.

Its present ***church***, the largest in Cornwall until Truro cathedral was completed in 1910, dates from Norman times and was built as the great church for an Augustinian priory founded here in 1162. Its west door, a series of seven receding arches, is considered one of the finest examples of Norman church architecture in Britain. The twin towers date from the 13th and 15th centuries, and inside there are a number of striking monuments, most notably that to Edward Eliot, which is considered to be one of the most impressive 18th century examples of its kind in Cornwall.

The Eliot family, now the earls of St Germans, acquired the priory shortly after the Dissolution of the Monasteries (1539) and renamed their new estate ***'Port Eliot'***. The present house, with its Gothic-looking turrets, is largely 19th century, although it incorporates fragments of the medieval monastic buildings. The grounds were laid out in the late 18th century by Humphry Repton, but are not open to the public.

Another of St Germans' exceptional buildings, Sir William Moyle's ***almshouses***, can be seen on the approaches to the village. Constructed in 1538 and carefully restored in the 1950's, the row is built to an unusual design, with prominent gables and a long first-floor balcony which is reached by a sturdy external staircase. A good view of the massive 13-arched viaduct which carries the main London-to-Penzance line over the estuary of the River Tiddy and can be seen from the former Victorian river port of ***St Germans' Quay***.

Ashton

Map 3 ref Q7

9 miles N of Torpoint off the A390

A group of interesting hidden places can be found within a few miles of each other, six miles upstream from the spectacular twin bridges over the River Tamar at Saltash. One of the most appealing National Trust properties in England can be found buried in the lanes to the east of the A388 Saltash-to-Callington road. ***Cotehele House*** is a low granite manor house set around three courtyards, which was largely built in Tudor times by Sir Richard Edgcumbe and his son, Piers.

In the 1550's, the family moved their main residence southwards to Mount Edgcumbe, a more accessible site overlooking Plymouth Sound; since then, Cotehele has been left relatively unaltered, except for the addition of the semi-fortified northwest tower in 1627. Inside, the Tudor great hall contains a remarkable collection of early

Cotehele House

armour and weaponry, and there are some exceptional tapestries and period furniture in the other rooms. The house incorporates some charming individual features, including a secret spy-hole to the great hall, a private chapel, and a tower clock with a bell, but no face or hands, which is believed to be the oldest working example of its kind in Britain.

The grounds of Cotehele House are some of the most delightful in the West Country. Above the house, there is an enclosed formal garden with a wide, shallow pond - below it, the ground falls away in a steep-sided combe which contains a spectacular collection of mature rhododendrons, azaleas and other flowering shrubs.

The garden's most enchanting feature - a medieval stone dovecote with a domed roof - stands beside a deep stream-fed pool between the house and the Tamar. At the foot of the combe, a tiny chapel stands on a promontory, 70 feet above the river's edge. This was built in the 15th century by Sir Richard Edgcumbe, a Lancastrian, to show thanks for his escape from the Yorkist forces of Richard III who had been pursuing him through Cotehele woods. Edgcumbe avoided capture by placing a stone in his cap and throwing it into the fast-flowing waters of the Tamar, a ploy which made his pursuers think he had jumped to his death. (He then went on to fight for Henry VII at Bosworth Field, and was knighted for his loyalty to the Tudors).

Cotehele was once a large working estate with its own flour mill, cider press, smithy and workshops; now restored to working order, these lie in a valley half a mile away from the main house and are open to visitors. Similarly, ***Cotehele Quay*** was once a significant river port with its own wharves, warehouses and lime kilns. Several of its once-derelict 18th and 19th century buildings have been given new life: one houses a branch of the ***National Maritime Museum***, while another is an excellent tearoom.

Calstock — *Map 3 ref Q7*

10 miles NE of Torpoint off the B3257

From Cotehele Quay it's a pleasant three-quarter-mile stroll through the woods to the former mining port of Calstock. This curious small town is dominated by a mighty ***railway viaduct*** which was one of the first in the country to be constructed of concrete blocks. It continues to carry trains travelling between Plymouth and Gunnislake along the picturesque ***Tamar Valley line***, a stretch of railway whose opening in 1907 ironically sounded the death knell for the traditional activities of the tow, for prior to this, Calstock had been the place where vast quantities of tin, granite and copper ore had been brought for loading onto barges bound for the coast and beyond. The town once has a flourishing boat-building industry, and was surrounded by mine-workings, spoil heaps and mineral railways. Tamar canoe expeditions can be commenced here. The picturesque churchyard of the restored 15th century parish ***Church of St Andrew***, at the top of Church Hill, contains the graves of many who perished in local mine accidents; inside, there are several memorials to the Edgcumbes of Cotehele.

Gunnislake — *Map 3 ref Q7*

12 miles NE of Torpoint off the B3257

The Tamar bends extravagantly on its way past Devon's Morwellham Quay to Gunnislake, the northern terminus of the ***Tamar Valley railway line***. Like Calstock, this is a former mining centre and river port which rises steeply from the western bank of the Tamar.

In the 1520's, Sir Piers Edgcumbe of Cotehele built Gunnislake's *'new'* bridge, a striking 180 foot long seven-arched granite structure which continues to serve as one of the main gateways to Cornwall. Indeed, it was the lowest bridging point on the Tamar for over 400 years (until the Plymouth-to-Saltash road bridge was completed in 1961), a feature which made it the scene of bitter fighting during the English Civil War.

Like many of its neighbours whose prosperity depended on the output from local mines, Gunnislake suffered a century of decline before undergoing a modest recovery in the last third of the 20th century. Today it is a pleasant small town with a number of attractive houses and inns.

Kit Hill *Map 3 ref P6*

12 miles NW of Torpoint off the A390

To the west of Gunnislake, the A390 passes along the southern edge of Kit Hill, a 1,090 foot peak which offers an outstanding view across southeast Cornwall to Plymouth Sound. On the summit stands the dramatic outline of an 80 foot chimney stack which was built in 1858 to serve one of the area's many copper mines. The 500 acre site was donated to the county in 1985 by Prince Charles, the Duke of Cornwall; it is rich in industrial remains and has recently been designated a country park.

Callington *Map 3 ref P7*

10 miles NW of Torpoint off the A388

This pleasant old market town nestling between the Rivers Tamar and Lynher lies at the heart of the fertile fruit growing country which is bordered by Dartmoor to the east and Bodmin Moor to the west, the very area which, for a few decades during the Victorian era, became the scene of frantic mining activity.

Dupath *Map 3 ref P7*

11 miles NW of Torpoint off the A388

This lovely village is home to an interesting 15th century chapel and well-house enclosing ***Dupath Well***, and an impressive Iron Age fort known as ***Cadson Bury*** standing on an oval hilltop site above the River Lynher, to the south of the A390.

Polbathic *Map 3 ref P9*

5 miles W of Torpoint off the A374

Set in 10 acres of mature Cornish gardens, ***Sconner House*** was originally built in the 1700's by the Cornwallis family - Admiral

Cornwallis was famed as one of Nelson's *'Band of Brothers'* at Trafalgar. Carefully converted to an hotel in the 1960's, it has recently undergone a complete renovation. Located at the gateway to the spectacular Rame Peninsula, Sconner House overlooks St Germans Estuary, a designated area of outstanding natural beauty and of particular interest to bird-watchers. Each of the eight spacious guest bedrooms is individually furnished and affords a marvellous view into the gardens or across the Estuary. Guests can take a Cornish cream tea in the handsome conservatory; the lively bar offers real

Sconner House Inn

ales and a wide range of malt whiskies. In the a la carte restaurant, head chef David Simpson prepares the best in traditional English cuisine, featuring the local fish and produce. Leisure facilities at nearby Whitsand Bay Hotel are availabe to Sconner House guests free of charge; there are also several magnificent golf courses in the area. Manager Alan Collins and his welcoming, efficient staff help to make a stay at this superior hotel a memorable experience. *Sconner House Inn, Polbathic, Nr Torpoint, Cornwall PL11 3ET Tel/Fax: 01503 230297.*

Saltash

Map 3 ref Q8

2½ miles N of Torpoint off the A38

Saltash's near-perpendicular streets feature many buildings of interest, including the 17th century ***Guildhall*** and ***Mary Newman's cottage*** (home of Mrs Francis Drake). Tamar River cruises depart from here. Brunel's ***Iron Railway Bridge*** opened in 1859, and the suspension road bridge in 1961.

Saltash Galleries

Saltash Galleries on the high street in Saltash features works by local artists covering a wide range of artistic styles and media. Crafts on offer include china figurines, stationery, Portmeiron and Spode china, Caithness glassware, Lilliput Lane model cottages, jewellery, pewterware, lamps and a superb variety of cards, ornaments and giftware. A winding spiral staircase leads upstairs to the welcoming and cosy tea shop/restaurant, where you can enjoy tasty hot and cold snacks, sandwiches, home-made cakes, cream teas and a range of teas, coffees, milkshakes and other drinks while admiring the paintings and other artworks that adorn the walls. In fine weather you might want to take refreshment on the outdoor veranda. *Saltash Galleries, 96 Fore Street, Saltash, Cornwall PL12 6JW Tel: 01752 846415.*

Notter Bridge, Near Saltash

Map 3 ref P8

2½ miles NW of Torpoint off the A38

Crylla Valley Cottages comprise a range of 20 traditionally built and characterful award winning cottages set in an area of outstanding natural beauty alongside the beautiful River Lynher. The cottages are surrounded by flower gardens, spacious lawns and handsome woodlands. Wildlife abounds and the site's 18 acres proffer a wide variety of wildflowers and plants, and sunchairs and garden seats throughout the grounds - a truly relaxed and relaxing environment. There is a secluded play area for younger visitors, a play lawn

Crylla Valley Cottages

equipped for badminton, volleyball and swingball, and an assortment of indoor board games available for all. Sleeping from four to eight guests, each cottage and bungalow is decorated and furnished to the highest standard, with every modern convenience and affording superb valley views. The atmosphere is welcoming and secluded; each cottage and bungalow offering all the privacy and comfort of high quality self-catering accommodation. Situated within easy access of a vast range of activities and attractions throughout the region, including Looe, Polperro, Plymouth, miles of sandy beaches at Cawsands and Whitsands and many other coastal resorts, handsome parks, gardens, historic homes and a superb range of eateries and pubs, the peace and seclusion of Crylla Valley is an ideal choice for an excellent base from which to explore the region. Open all year round. Highly commended by the ETB. *Crylla Valley Cottages, Notter Bridge, Nr Saltash, Cornwall PL12 4RN Tel: 01752 851133 Fax 01752 851666.*

Lostwithiel

This attractive small market town stands at the head of the Fowey estuary at the historic lowest bridging point on the river. One of Cornwall's medieval Stannary towns, tin and other raw metals were brought here for assaying and onward shipping until upstream mining activity caused the anchorage to silt up, forcing the port to move down-river to the estuary mouth. Present-day Lostwithiel is an atmospheric touring and angling centre whose long history has left it with a legacy of interesting old buildings, many of which are set in characteristic narrow alleyways, or opes. The remains of the 13th century great hall which served as the treasury and stannary offices can be seen in Quay Street, and in Fore Street there is a fine example of an early 18th century arcaded ***Guildhall*** which now serves as the civic museum. The nearby municipal offices date from later in the century, as does the old grammar school in Queen Street, and elsewhere in the town there are some fine Georgian residences and shop fronts. ***The old malt house*** is worth finding for its unusual plaque, declaring *'Walter Kendal founded this house and hath a lease for 3,000 years beginning 29 September 1652.'*

Lostwithiel's 14th century parish ***Church of St Bartholomew*** has a rare octagonal spire; one of only six in the county, its style is reminiscent of the church architecture of northern France. Another unusual feature is the row of upper windows in the aisle, or clerestory, which is one of only four in Cornwall. The early 14th century font is unusually large and richly carved. During the Civil War, the Parliamentarians made this the focus for their anti-Royalist feeling when they brought a horse into the church and provocatively christened it Charles *'in contempt of his sacred Majesty'*.

Duchy Coffee Shop is a cosy, welcoming establishment located down a quiet lane here in the scenic village of Lostwithiel. Friendly, accommodating owners Fiona and Hans Lal make every effort to

Dutchy Coffee Shop

make every customer's visit to this agreeable coffee shop both pleasant and relaxing. The superior menu boasts a range of cakes, breads, teacakes, delicious snacks and hot and cold dishes, all home-made by Fiona's mother. Popular with local residents, walkers and boating enthusiasts, all of whom enjoy the warm and informal atmosphere, the Duchy offers tasty treats and a variety of coffees, teas and other hot and cold drinks. Open Monday to Saturday all year round, and on Sundays during the summer months, when visitors can enjoy a full Sunday lunch. *Duchy Coffee Shop, 10 Fore Street, Lostwithiel, Cornwall PL22 0BW Tel: 01208 873184 Fax: 01579 363669.*

The spectacular National Trust-owned property, ***Lanhydrock House***, lies midway between the A38 and B3269 north of Lostwithiel. Prior to the Dissolution of the Monasteries, the 400 acre estate belonged to Bodmin's Augustinian priory of St Petroc, then in 1620 it was acquired by the Robartes family, in whose possession it remained until it passed to the National Trust in 1953. The house is set in a superb position in the valley of the River Fowey and is approached

Lanhydrock House

along an avenue of sycamore and beech trees, some of which were originally planted over three centuries ago. Visitors pass through an imposing 17th century gatehouse which, along with the north wing, is one of the few parts of the original structure to have escaped the fire which tore through the building in 1881.

Thankfully, the magnificent first floor gallery in the north wing survived; over 115 feet long, it is illuminated by broad mullioned windows and contains a remarkable plasterwork ceiling showing scenes from the Old Testament which is believed to be the work of the Abbott family, master plasterers of North Devon.

Because of the fire, most of Lanhydrock House is a Victorian reconstruction built in the 1880s to the original 17th century design. The updated interior contains a maze of comfortably appointed rooms, over 40 of which are now open to the public. Highlights include the estate offices, servants' quarters, buttery and nursery, which together create a unique picture of life in an opulent Victorian country mansion. The grounds contain an attractive woodland shrubbery, and a much-photographed formal garden and parterre which is overlooked by the small estate church of St Hyderoc.

A mile and a half downstream, the imposing Norman keep of ***Restormel Castle*** stands on a promontory overlooking the wooded valley of the River Fowey. The fortress was built in the early 12th century by Edmund, Earl of Cornwall, and is remarkably well preserved for its age. The walls of the massive circular shell are 30 feet high in places, and the whole structure is surrounded by a deep dry moat which is lined with flowers in spring. The castle was in use until the 16th century, and was reoccupied for a time by Parliamentarian forces during the English Civil War. Now under the care of English Heritage, visitors can climb a series of walkways onto the ramparts. The road to the south passes close to the site of a disused mine which was once the largest source of iron ore in Cornwall. Material was transported from here by tramway to Lostwithiel, and then by barge to Fowey for loading onto seagoing vessels. ***Bradock Down***, to the east, was the site of a famous Royalist victory.

Around Lostwithiel

Luxulyan — *Map 2 ref L8*

4 miles SW of Lostwithiel off the A390

Luxulyan is the location of the remarkable ***Treffry Viaduct***. Over 100 feet high and 200 yards long, it was built in 1842 to carry mineral ores, quarried stone and fresh water to the newly-created port of Par.

The countryside east of the Fowey estuary contains some exceptionally attractive rural backwaters, including Lerryn, Couch's Mill and St Veep. The church at St Winnow has an impressive 15th century stained-glass window and one of Cornwall's few rood screens.

Par *Map 2 ref M9*

5 miles SW of Lostwithiel off the A3082

This 19th century port town is just a short distance from ***Lancrow Farmhouse***, a handsome and welcoming country stone-built holiday cottage set in a beautiful rural setting but less than a mile from easy access to Fowey, St Austell, Lostwithiel and the surrounding area. Marvellous beaches, National Trust properties and the Lost Gardens of Heligan are all within a short drive's distance away. Facilities for golfing, riding and sailing are also near at hand. From the farmhouse there is excellent walking through historic woodlands, and some breathtaking country scenery across 25 acres of grassland. The standard of accommodation at this restored Grade II listed 17th century Cornish Farmhouse is very high. The kitchen features a blue oil-fired Aga and a handsome pine dresser as well as a fridge

Lancrow Farmhouse

freezer and microwave; the comfortable, beamed sitting room has a wonderful granite fireplace. The open-plan dining room features a stunning long pine farmhouse table and pine dresser. There are three charming bedrooms, decorated with Laura Ashley prints and supremely comfortable furnishings. There is also a utility room with washing machine. Electricity and all linens are included in the price. No smoking. No dogs. *Lancrow Farmhouse, off Penpillick Hill, Nr Par, Cornwall PL24 2SA Tel/Fax: 01726 814263.*

Lanreath *Map 3 ref N8*

4 miles SE of Lostwithiel off the B3359

There is an interesting ***Museum of Rural Life*** here, which contains a unique collection of antique farm engines, tractors and agricultural implements. Much of the dense woodland surrounding the Fowey estuary is owned by the National Trust, and it was here that Kenneth Grahame discovered the glade that was to become the Wild Wood in his children's classic, *The Wind in the Willows*. It can be found along the path which runs north from the 16th century bridge at Lerryn.

Tredethick Farm Cottages are eight picturesque, award-winning stone-built self-catering cottages sleeping from two to six people and set in idyllic countryside between the scenic town of Lostwithiel and the picturesque village of Lerryn. Also within easy distance of Fowey, Polperro, St Austell, the National Trust property at Lanhydrock and the Lost Gardens of Heligan, these distinguished cottages offer the perfect base from which to explore many of the area's delights. Each charming cottage has its own distinct character; all provide easy access to meadows and woodland from the doorstep down to the river Fowey and the church of St Winnow, used in the series Poldark. There are three resident goats (Abbey, Mango and Chutney) on the farm, as well as a sheep called Henry

Tredethick Farm Cottages

and a pony called Gypsy, who is happy to take young children on sedate rides. The cottages offer many original features such as exposed beams, and combine traditional country cottage touches such as pine units and furnishings with every modern convenience. Two of the eight are designed to be wheelchair-friendly. No smoking. All linen provided. Games room. Baby-sitting service. Two barbecue areas. *Tredethick Farm Cottages, The Guildhouse, Tredethick, Lostwithiel, Cornwall PL22 0LE Tel/Fax: 01208 873618.*

Lerryn

Map 2 ref N8

3 miles SE of Lostwithiel off the B3359

The Ship Inn is a welcoming Free House located in the centre of the unspoilt riverside village of Lerryn. This cosy, whitewased establishment dates back to the early 1600's, and offers a range of real ales, malt whiskies and wines, and traditional home cooking. In cooler weather visitors can enjoy the log fire; in the warmer months the handome garden is the perfect place to relax. The food on offer is excellent, featuring a range of some 40 home-cooked pies using local produce. A sample of these tempting pies includes Winchester chicken, venison, pheasant and Madeira, lamb and honey,

The Ship Inn

and pork and cider. There is an extensive selection of vegetarian meals. Handy for walks in the nearby woods, or a boat trip on the river - at the winter solstice there's a special boat race; a river treasure hunt marks the summer solstice - the quiet beaches and coves of the south coast are close by, as are cycling and walking trails, recreation centres and many of the historic treasures of the area, such as Truro Cathedral, Plymouth Hoe, and Restormel Castle. *The Ship Inn, Lerryn, Lostwithiel, Cornwall PL22 0PT Tel: 01208 872374.*

Golant

Map 2 ref M9

2½ miles S of Lostwithiel off the B3269

The B3269 road to Golant passes the remarkable ***Tristan stone***, a 6th century standing stone which is inscribed in Latin. This 7 foot monolith is believed to have come from ***Castle Dore***, a circular Iron Age fort lying close to the turning to Golant which was occupied periodically until the 6th century.

Golant itself is a delightful waterside community whose small early 16th century church, St Samson's, contains an unusual wooden pulpit made of medieval bench ends; an ancient holy well lies beneath the south porch.

The return journey to St Austell passes close to ***Tregrehan***, an attractive woodland garden which has been developed since the early 19th century by the Carlyon family. Specialising in rare species from warm-temperate regions, the garden incorporates a walled garden, a series of glasshouses and a small nursery.

Bellscat Guest House is a strikingly beautiful white stuccoed Georgian farmhouse built on a slight knoll. From this elevated position it enjoys views across the estuary and into wooded countryside, with the charming hamlet of St Winnow beyond. Surrounded by rolling pastureland and fields running down to the water's edge, this distinguished establishment offers two double-bed guest bedrooms, each with private bath or shower room. The northern boundary of the property is marked by a scenic tree-edged tidal inlet. The surrounding area offers excellent walking along the many lovely coastal footpaths, a range of National Trust properties and other places of interest and, as might be expected, facilities for sail-

Bellscat Guest House

ing and a variety of water sports, along the picturesque tree-lined estuaries or the open seas. The nearby riverside village of Golant features a 13th century church, village post office and shop, a good pub and a fine restaurant. Fowey and Par are just three miles away, while Carlyon Bay and golf course are only four miles' distant. No children under 12. No pets. No smoking. *Bellscat, Golant, Fowey, Cornwall PL23 1LA Tel: 01726 833404.*

Fowey

Map 2 ref M9

5 miles S of Lostwithiel off the B3269

The lovely old port and historic seafaring town of Fowey (pronounced Foy) guards the western entrance to the river from which it takes its name. The narrow lanes and alleyways of the old town rise abruptly from the water's edge in a pleasant mixture of architectural styles from Elizabethan to Edwardian.

The deep water harbour has been used as an anchorage for sea-going vessels since the time of the ancient Romans, and china clay continues to be exported from the whitened jetties which lie half a mile or so upstream. The town's long history is closely linked with its maritime traditions. During the Hundred Years War, local mariners recruited to fight the French became known as the *'Fowey Gallants'*; some refused to disband, and instead formed a notorious gang of pirates who would attack any vessel straying too close to this stretch of coast. Following a devastating French raid in 1457, a chain was stretched across the estuary mouth at night to deter hostile ships from entering the harbour.

Present-day Fowey is a peaceful community which is connected by vehicle ferry to Bodinnick on the eastern bank, and by passenger ferry to Polruan. The harbour is filled with pleasure craft from all over Britain and continental Europe, and there a number of fine old buildings which are worth closer inspection, for example the ***Noah's Ark Museum***, housed in one of the oldest structures in Fowey, the medieval town hall in Trafalgar Square, which is occupied by another interesting local museum, and the Ship Inn, a part-15t -century building with a Victorian facade which was once the town house of the Rashleigh family.

Millstream Pottery is an attractive establishment selling a wide range of hand-crafted decorative and practical giftware. Pieces by local artisans are crafted to the highest standard, using glazes in rich blues, greens and other colours - there is also a special glaze associated with Millstream itself. In addition to these individual and exclusive items are a variety of baskets, candlesticks, candleholders and other decorative pieces as well as cards, ornaments, tableware and other superb gift ideas. Visitors to this marvellous shop can watch as individual pieces are 'thrown', shaped and crafted on the potter's wheel. Owner Mrs G Histon takes pride in continuing Cornwall's fine tradition in the arts and crafts, and this handsome shop is a testament to that legacy. *Millstream Pottery, 19 North Street, Fowey, Cornwall PL23 1DB Tel: 01726 832512.*

Millstream Pottery

Old Quay House is a delightful family hotel located on its own quay overlooking the River Fowey. Originally a seaman's mission built in 1890, it was converted to an hotel in 1950 and offers nine spacious, light and airy guestrooms, four with spectacular sea views. The superb dinner menu changes daily and makes use of fresh, local produce. Cream teas and lunches are also available, and can be taken outdoors on the spacious veranda affording marvellous views. Close to Heligan Gardens and all the charms of Fowey itself, this handsome establishment offers a welcome and comfortable stay for guests looking for an active holiday or just the perfect place to relax and unwind. *Old Quay House Hotel, 28 Fore Street, Fowey, Cornwall PL23 1AQ Tel: 01726 833302 Fax: 01726 833668 email dean.rodgers@lineone.net*

The Old Quay House

The Rashleigh family seat, ***Menabilly***, lies to the southeast of the town and was subsequently the home of Daphne du Maurier, who used the setting - rechristened *'Manderley'* - in her famous novel, Rebecca. Another of Fowey's literary residents was the Cornish novelist Sir Arthur Quiller-Couch, who lived for over 50 years at the Haven on the Esplanade. There are some excellent beaches nearby.

CHAPTER THREE
Mid-Cornwall North

Newquay Beach

Chapter 3 - Area Covered

For precise location of places please refer to the colour maps found at the rear of the book.

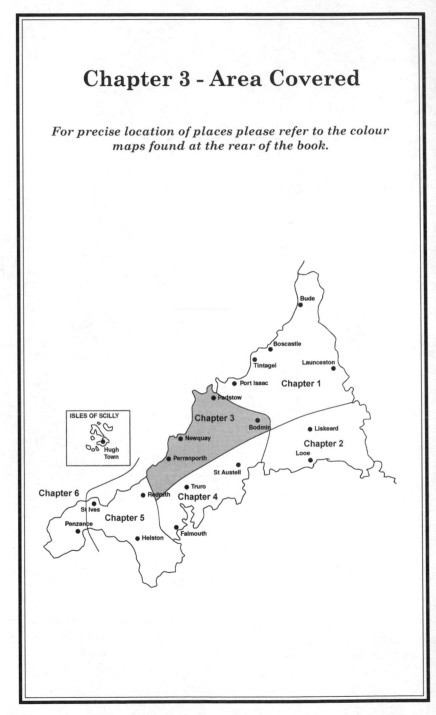

3
Mid-Cornwall North

Introduction

Fleets of trawlers, netters and crabbers, colourful harbours surrounded by pastel-washed houses, miles of fine sandy beaches and rugged cliffs - the towns and villages of this part of north Cornwall offer visitors some of the most typically Cornish scenes and experiences. Narrow streets run down to bustling waterfronts, where fishing boats rub gunnels with cabin cruisers and yachts, and visitors can watch the ebb and flow of harbour life.

Home to the historic towns of Padstow, Bodmin, Newquay and St Agnes, and the picturesque coves and villages along the coast and further inland, this region of Cornwall is a treasure trove of quiet bays, lively and popular resorts, and fabulous walks along the renowned ***Camel Trail***, which follows the winding path of the Camel Estuary.

Padstow

For many centuries, Padstow's sheltered position on the western side of the Camel estuary has made it a welcome haven for vessels seeking shelter from the perils of the north Cornish coast. However, the silting of the river in the 19th century created a new hazard for shipping, the evocatively named ***Doom Bar***, which restricted entry to the estuary mouth and effectively spelled the end for the ancient settlement as a major port.

Once the ecclesiastical capital of Cornwall, the town's name is derived from St Petroc, the Irish missionary saint who landed here from Wales in the 6th century. The ***parish church*** is dedicated to him, although the present building dates from the 13th and 14th centuries; inside there is a striking Elizabethan pulpit and some comical bench ends, one of which depicts a fox preaching to a gaggle of geese. St Petroc also founded a monastery here, but in the 10th century it was moved to Bodmin to protect its occupants from Viking raids.

Padstow's original monastery is believed to have stood on the site of the present-day Prideaux Place, a handsome Elizabethan mansion at the top of the town which was built in the 1580s by the Prideaux family. Still occupied by descendants of the original owners, the house is set in extensive grounds incorporating a 20 acre deer park and formal Italianate garden. Highlights of the interior include the library, drawing room and great chamber with its fine plasterwork ceiling. Several monuments to the Prideaux family can be seen in the parish church.

With its narrow alleyways and tightly packed slate-hung buildings, Padstow's old quarter retains much of its medieval character. The harbour still supports a sizable fishing fleet and is enhanced by the addition of floodgates which retain the sea water at low tide. The area around the old port contains a number of interesting old buildings, including the 15th century ***Merchants' Guild House*** on the north quay, and the 16th century ***Court House*** of Sir Walter Raleigh on the south quay; the latter was used by Sir Walter's agents for collecting Stannary taxes.

Today, Padstow's harbour and nearby shopping streets throng with visitors throughout the summer, some of whom arrive along the beautiful ***Camel cycle path*** which follows the course of the old railway line from Wadebridge; the long curved bridge which crosses the mouth of Little Petherick creek is one of its highlights. The ***Padstow Shipwreck Museum*** is also well worth a visit.

One of Padstow's great traditions is the festival of the *'ObbyOss'*, a boisterous street celebration with origins going back to pagan times whose modern observance still makes little concession to outsiders. (The Obby Oss is a ferocious figure with a primitive mask, tall conical hat, flat circular body and sailcloth skirt.) Throughout the day on May 1, rival Osses are led on a wild dance through the narrow thoroughfares of Padstow by a staff-wielding *'Teaser'* to the accompaniment of traditional music and singing. This ancient ritual, with its strong undertones of pagan fertility rites, is believed to be one of the oldest celebrations of its kind in Europe.

Among the fine beaches in Padstow are those at ***St George's Well*** and ***Trevone Bay***. The Camel Trail makes for excellent walking, and follows a former railway line.

Originally built as a coaching inn, ***The White Hart*** occupies a Grade II listed 16th century building - one of the oldest in Padstow. It has been carefully and comprehensively restored, and now offers, in the former stables which overlook the attractive garden, the highest standards in comfortable self-catering accommodation. This charming, evocative establishment retains many original features, such as the exposed beams, but also incorporates modern amenities such as a dishwasher, and all the other conveniences visitors have come to expect.

The White Hart

The apartment, located on the first floor, offers accommodation for two people, with one double bedroom, sitting room, kitchen and shower room. Two more people can be accommodated in the additional double bedroom and en suite bathroom on the ground floor. These facilities are completely self-contained, with a locked entrance so that guests are free to come and go as they please. All linens and towels provided. There is a charming first-floor sundeck for guests' use. English Tourist Board Highly Commended. Luxurious bedrooms with en suite bathrooms available for bed and breakfast. Proprietor Patricia Jacoby makes every effort to ensure her guests have a very pleasant and memorable stay. *The White Hart, 1 New Street, Padstow, Cornwall PL28 8EA Tel: 01841 532350 Fax: 01841 533553.*

The Golden Lion

The Golden Lion in Padstow is an appealing and homely public house offering a range of traditional ales as well as tempting bar snacks. These fine refreshments can be taken in front of a roaring fire in the original stone fireplace, or outdoors in the attractive beer garden. Snacks on offer include fresh crab and other local catches, ploughman's meals, basket meals, steaks and jacket potatoes. The pub's quiet village location near the sea is tranquil and relaxing. Owners Lorraine and Alex Rickard are the convivial and attentive hosts. The Golden Lion also offers accommodation in its three spacious and welcoming guest bedrooms. *The Golden Lion, Lanadwell Street, Padstow, Cornwall PL28 8AN Tel: 01841 532797.*

Around Padstow

Rock — *Map 2 ref K6*

1 mile NE of Padstow off the B3314

This former fishing village has a collection of Georgian, Victorian and more recent residences, most of which are occupied for just a few months each summer. A passenger ferry plies back and forth across the Camel estuary from the quay to Padstow, as it has done for centuries. In recent years the village has become renowned as a watersports centre, with its own sailing and wind-surfing school. In common with the church at St Enodoc, St Michael's church at nearby Porthilly has had to be regularly retrieved from unwelcome sand drifts.

St Merryn — *Map 2 ref J6*

2 miles W of Padstow off the B3276

Here in this placid and picturesque village, ***Treginegar Guest House*** is a charming and picturesque stone-built bed and breakfast and self-catering establishment offering a warm, welcoming and relaxing haven. After standing derelict for nine years, this handsome

Treginegar Guest House

building was given a new lease on life in 1996 when it was carefully and conscientiously converted into a homely and supremely comfortable family-run guest house offering four attractive guest rooms; in addition there are large holiday bungalows to let for self-catering. Situated in splendid and peaceful rural surroundings, with access locally to seven bays, golfing, bird watching, superb walking, riding and other outdoor pursuits, Treginegar has a licensed bar and restaurant offering the best in fresh local produce, including locally-landed fish and seafood dishes. Honoured with 2 Crowns by the English Tourist Board, this former farmhouse makes a cosy and genial base from which to sample all that the surrounding area has to offer. Visitors return again and again for the hospitality and service the Treginegar provides. *Treginegar Guest House, St Merryn, Near Padstow, Cornwall PL28 8PT Tel: 01841 521042.*

Just a short distance from the village, and less than a mile from Harlyn Bay, one of the most beautiful sandy beaches on the North Cornwall coast, ***Higher Harlyn Park*** caravan park is ideally situated. The Park consists of many fields, catering for touring vans and all kinds of camping. Electrical hook-ups are available and the facilities include a fully stocked shop, heated outdoor swimming pool, toilet blocks with hot showers, hairdryers and a lauderette. There are also a number of static caravans available for hire, fully equipped with shower, toilet, cooker, fridge and colour television (early booking is highly recommended). Also on site is a pub, *'Ye Olde Barne'*, with three bars and a welcoming ambience. Above there's a restaurant for morning and evening meals. Padstow is only 10 minutes

Higher Harlyn Park

away, where visitors can enjoy a variety of watersports. With all this, excellent walking and cycling routes and many first-class golf courses nearby, Higher Harlyn Park makes an ideal base from which to explore the delights of the area. *Higher Harlyn Park, St Merryn, Padstow, Cornwall PL28 8SG Tel: 01841 520022/520879 Fax: 01841 520942.*

St Issey — *Map 2 ref K6*

3 miles S of Padstow off the A389

In the church at St Issey, the altar canopy incorporates a striking collection of carved Catacleuse stone figures which are thought to have once formed part of a chest tomb. There is also a remarkable early photograph of 1869, showing the church tower collapsing with a top-hatted policeman looking haplessly on. At nearby Tredissick there's an interesting Shire Horse Centre.

In October 1842 whilst visiting Padstow, Charles Dickens was greatly inspired and penned his wonderful and moving tale, *A Christmas Carol*, in which he mentions Tinnens Cottages and a lighthouse (Trevose). His good friend Dr Miles Marley, whose son Dr Henry Frederick Marley practised in Padstow for 51 years, provided Dickens with a surname for Scrooge's deceased partner, Jacob. In this heart-warming story Dickens reworks an idea that began as an interlude in *The Pickwick Papers*, where Gabriel Grub is plainly recognisable as the prototype of the grasping Ebenezer Scrooge. Dr Henry Frederick Marley died on 27th January, 1908, aged 76 years, in his home in Mellingey, St Issey - the service at St Issey Church was read by the Reverend W J Wyon.

The Dickens connection lives on today in ***The Pickwick Inn***, a family-run Free House here in St Issey, overlooking the beautiful Camel Estuary and in an area of outstanding natural beauty. Here on sunny days guests can enjoy a hearty meal and refreshing drink *'al fresco'* - an ideal stop-off point for walkers and cyclists. There is a safe adveture playground, a large well-lit car park, as well as tennis, lawn bowls and poolside barbeques. Reservations are advised

The Pickwick Inn

for the intimate candle-lit restaurant, which offers fine dining and an excellent choice of wines from around the wprld. For every generation The Pickwick Inn is a Dickens of a pub. *The Pickwick Inn and Restaurant, Burgois, St Issey, Nr Padstow, Cornwall PL27 7QQ tel: 01841 540361.*

Wadebridge

Map 2 ref L6

7 miles SE of Padstow off the A39

This ancient port and busy market town stands at the historic lowest bridging point on the Camel (a bypass to the north now carries the A39 over the river). At 320 feet, the town's medieval 14 arched road bridge is one of the longest in Cornwall. Originally composed of 17 arches, it was built in the 15th century by the local priest to convey his flock across the river in safety. It is still known by its traditional name, the ***'Bridge on Wool'***, for reasons that are unclear: either it was paid from by wealthy local wool merchants, or its foundations were laid on bales of raw wool, an absorbent material which solidifies when soaked and compressed. Once a thriving river port and railway town, Wadebridge is now a tranquil place with a good selection of shops. Each June, the ***Royal Cornwall Show*** is held in the county showground, a mile west of the centre. Wadebridge is also home to the ***John Betjeman Centre***, a tribute to the man and his works, and hosts an annual folk festival.

Located on a handsome street in the pedestrianised shopping precinct of the town, ***Victoria Antiques*** is an extensive and distinguished shop occupying 5,000 square feet and three floors, making it the largest retail outlet in Cornwall. This impressive establishment offers a very wide range of handsome antiques: from furnishings - period pieces, old pine furniture, dressers, cabinets,

Victoria Antiques

tables, over 400 chairs, writing desks, fire screens and fire surrounds, dressing tables, bookcases - to barometers, clocks (including some fine grandfather clocks), mirrors, china, stuffed animals, model ships and teapots. Each piece is distinctive and attractive. With over 20 years' experience in the antiques trade, owners Mike and Sylvia Daly can offer expert advice and excellent service. *Victoria Antiques, 21 Molesworth Street, Wadebridge, Cornwall PL27 7DH Tel: 01208 814160.*

To the west of Wadebridge, the A39 leads up onto the ***St Breock Downs***, the site of such striking Bronze Age remains as the ancient ***St Breock Longstone*** and ***Nine Maidens stone row***.

Washaway — *Map 2 ref L7*

10 miles SE of Padstow off the A389

One of the loveliest country manor houses in the West Country can be found on the eastern side of the A389 Bodmin road. ***Pencarrow House*** lies hidden in a 50 acre wooded estate which encompasses an Iron Age encampment and a beautiful woodland garden with a lake, ice house, Victorian granite rockery, and American and Italianate gardens. The grounds also contain an internationally renowned collection of conifers and over 500 species of rhododendron. The interior of the Georgian house is furnished with some outstanding 18th century paintings, period furniture and china.

Bodmin — *Map 2 ref M7*

8 miles SE of Padstow off the A389

Bustling by day, yet quiet by night, the historic former county town of Bodmin lies midway between Cornwall's north and south coasts at the junction of two ancient cross-country trading routes.

For many centuries, traders between Wales, Ireland and northern France preferred the overland route between the Camel and Fowey estuaries to the hazardous sea journey around Land's End. ***Castle Canyke*** to the southeast of the town was built during the Iron Age to defend this important trade route, and a few centuries later the Romans erected a fort on a site above the River Camel to the west of the town, one of a string they built in the Southwest to defend strategic river crossings; the remains of a quadrilateral earthwork can still be made out today. The ancient cross-country route is now a waymarked footpath known as the Saints' Way.

Bodmin's most famous early visitor was perhaps St Petroc, one of the most influential of the early Welsh missionary saints who landed in Cornwall in the 6th century. The monastery he founded near Padstow was moved to Bodmin in the 10th century to protect it from seaborne Viking raids; although it survived until the Dissolution of the Monasteries in 1539, little of it remains today. ***Bodmin's parish church***, perhaps the most impressive and definitely the largest in Cornwall, is dedicated to St Petroc. Rebuilt in the 15th century and renovated in the 19th, it contains a magnificent Norman font whose immense bowl is supported on five finely carved columns, and a priceless ivory casket in which the remains of the saint were placed in 1177, after they have been recovered from a light-fingered Augustinian monk.

Bodmin is also renowned for its holy wells - 11 in all. Some, such as ***Eye Water Well***, are known for their restorative properties, and some, such as ***St Guron's Well*** opposite the church, for being ancient places of baptism. Bodmin was the only market town in Cornwall to be mentioned in the Domesday Book, and at one time it boasted its own mint and, later, the county assizes. However, the 19th century rise of Truro as Cornwall's cathedral city stripped Bodmin of its county town status. A number of impressive relics of its former glory nevertheless remain, including the Tudor guildhall, the former court buildings, and the ***Turret Clock*** where former mayor, Nicholas Boyer, was hanged for his part in the Prayer Book Rebellion on 1549. Public executions were also held at ***Bodmin Gaol*** in Berrycombe Road, a once-feared place which now operates as an hotel and features a fascinating exhibition that takes in the former dungeons.

Bodmin also contains two first-rate museums: the ***Town Museum***, and the ***Regimental Museum*** (also known as the Duke of Cornwall' Light Infantry Museum), which is housed in the Duke of Cornwall's old headquarters. Turf Street leads up past ***Mount Folly*** to ***the Beacon***, a scenic picnic area with a 140 foot obelisk at its summit which was built to commemorate the Victorian general, Sir Walter Raleigh Gilbert. One of Britain's earliest railways was opened in 1830 to link Bodmin with the Camel estuary at Wadebridge. In recent years the track has been reopened as a public cyclepath and walkway, ***The Camel Trail***, which runs all the way from Boscarne Junction to Padstow.

Dunmere View is an attractive modern house offering bed and breakfast accommodation less than a mile from Bodmin town cen-

Dunmere View

tre. This handsome home offers two guest bedrooms and a welcoming lounge with open fire. There is also a snooker room. The surrounding garden and open countryside make for superb unspoilt views and some excellent walking; there are also pony rides available for children. The rooms are tastefully decorated, and there is a jacuzzi bath for visitors' enjoyment. The full English breakfast caters for all tastes - vegetarians and anyone requiring a special menu are welcome to ring in advance with their request. Proprietor Debbie Marshall is the welcoming and conscientious host; she makes every effort to ensure that guests have an enjoyable and relaxing stay. This distinguished B&B is near the Camel Trail, golf courses, moors and the coast - an excellent base from which to explore the riches of the area. *Dunmere View, Higher Bodiniel Road, Bodmin, Cornwall PL31 2PD Tel: 01208 76482/0421 570208.*

The Hole in the Wall pub and restaurant in Bodmin is a charming and welcoming establishment dating back to 1700, when it was a debtors' prison. Adorned with memorabilia from around the world - old military weapons, hats, rifles, swords, masks, firemen's helmets, medals and regimental badges - this CAMRA-recommended pub offers a wide variety of real ales, including regular guest ales, and a range of delicious snacks and meals making use of locally available produce, steaks and seafood. This cosy pub is just the place for a relaxing drink and great food in a warm and comfortable atmosphere. Access from Dennison Road carpark to the secluded pub courtyard. Open Monday-Saturday 11.30-2.30 and 5-11, Sun 12-10.30. *The Hole in the Wall, 16 Crockwell Street, Bodmin, Cornwall PL31 2DS Tel: 01208 72397 Fax: 01208 76004 email: alanbarter@aol.com*

The Hole in the Wall

St Columb Major *Map 2 ref K7*

6 miles S of Padstow off the A39

Thankfully bypassed by the main road, the small town of St Columb Major was once considered as the location for Cornwall's cathedral (it lost out to Truro). The parish ***Church of St Columba*** is unusually large, with a four-tiered tower and a wide through-arch; inside there are some fine 16th and 17th century monumental brasses to the Arundell family. The church is adjoined to the south and east by handsome old residential buildings, creating something of the atmosphere of a cathedral close. The town is home to an annual music festival.

The Red Lion in Fore Street is renowned for its former landlord, James Polkinghorne, a famous exponent of Cornish wrestling who is depicted in action on a plaque on an external wall. Another of St Columb Major's inns, the Silver Ball Hotel, marks the town's other great sporting tradition, *'hurling the silver ball'*. This rowdy medieval game is played twice a year - on Shrove Tuesday and on the Saturday 11 days later - and involved two teams of several hundred people (the *'townsmen'* and the *'countrymen'*) who endeavour to carry a silver-painted ball made of apple wood through goals set two miles apart. Once a common pastime throughout the county, this ancient Cornish game is now only practised here and, in a less rumbustious form, at St Ives. Such is the passion for the St Columb event that windows of houses and shops in the locality have to be boarded up for the occasion.

St Columb Meadery offers guests a chance to wine and dine the medieval way. Located in the handsome Old Rectory here in St Columb Major, it is open all year round from 7 pm until 11 pm, and is a welcoming and enjoyable establishment offering a memorable evening dining, with a range of delicious meals for all the family. This licensed restaurant has a good stock of wines from the local Cornish Mead Company, which guests are welcome to savour with their meals, or to buy and take home with them as a souvenir of Cornwall and Cornish history.

Mead, which is made from honey, grapes, and other natural ingredients, was the first alcoholic beverage to be consumed in the great halls and palaces of Britain, dating back to the Middle Ages. The medieval custom of newlyweds drinking this honey wine for one month after their wedding ceremony has given us the word *'honeymoon'*. St Columb Meadery is one of seven Meadery restaurants first established in Cornwall some 30 years ago. They soon became popular with local people and holidaymakers alike. In common with

St Columb Meadery

the other six dotted throughout Cornwall, St Columb Meadery remains a family concern. *St Columb Meadery, The Old Rectory, St Columb Major, Cornwall, Tel: 01637 880110*

Two miles southeast of St Columb Major, the land rises to 700 feet above sea level on Castle Downs, site of the massive Iron Age hill fort known as ***Castle-an-Dinas***, whose three earthwork ramparts enclose an area of over six acres. The climb to the gorse-covered summit is rewarded with panoramic views over the leafy Vale of Lanherne to the northwest, and towards the unearthly landscape of the china clap spoil heaps to the south.

Screech Owl Sanctuary

To the South of St Columb Major and just off the main A30 lies ***Screech Owl Sanctuary***. The Sanctuary is a rescue centre providing care and rehabilitation for sick and injured owls, to ensure their safe release back into the wild when they are fully recovered or to provide them with a permanent home if they are permanently disabled. The Sanctuary's aims also include promoting awareness of the conservation needs of owl species.

Owners Tom and Caroline Screech and their dedicated, knowledgeable and friendly staff provide information on the building and siting of owl nest boxes to enhance the wild population of owls. Visitors are allowed to touch and see the owls at close proximity, and can take a guided tour of the centre. From time to time, lectures on owls and their habitats are given in the indoor Education Centre, accompanied by a selection of owls to see and touch. Owl husbandry and welfare courses are also available. There's a small tea room for snacks and a charming picnic area, as well as a small shop selling owl souvenirs and crafts. Open daily 10 a.m. - 6 p.m. Small admission charge. Free parking. *Screech Owl Sanctuary, Near Indian Queens, Goss Moor, St Columb, Cornwall TR9 6HP Tel: 01726 860182*

St Mawgan — *Map 2 ref J7*

4 miles SW of Padstow off the A39

This beautiful village lies submerged in the mature trees of the ***Vale of Lanherne***. The restored church has one of the finest collections of monumental brasses in the country; most are of the Arundell family, whose 13th century former manor house, Lanherne, was taken over by the closed Carmelite order of nuns in 1794. The churchyard contains a richly carved lantern cross dating from around 1420 and an extraordinary timber memorial in the shape of the stern of a boat, which is dedicated to the 10 souls who froze to death in their lifeboat after being shipwrecked off the coast in 1846. The village inn, the Falcon, is reputed to have been named during the Reformation, when it was the practice to release a bird into the air to signal that a secret Catholic mass was about to take place. On the coast at ***Mawgan Porth***, the remains of a Saxon settlement can be made out which once supported a small fishing and herding community. Various 9th to 11th century dwellings can be identified near the beach, along with the foundations of a larger courtyard house and the outline of a cemetery.

The coastline between Mawgan Porth and Padstow is among the most rugged and impressive in Cornwall. Near ***Park Head***, the sea has pounded the volcanic cliffs into a series of spectacular shapes known as the ***Bedruthan Steps*** after the ancient Cornish giant who is said to have used them as stepping stones. At high tide, the steps are lashed by the waves, but at low tide the water recedes to reveal a superb sandy beach which can only be accessed via a steep and perilous cliff path, which is often closed due to subsidence.

The Bonsai Nursery just on the outskirts of St Mawgan is a fascinating centre for the cultivation and study of these wonderful dwarf plants. Admission free.

Porthcothan *Map 2 ref J6*

3 miles SW of Padstow off the B3276

Much of the cliffscape around this former smugglers' haunt is owned by the National Trust; a bit further north, the view of the Atlantic is particularly dramatic around ***Constantine Bay*** and ***Trevose Head***.

Newquay

A settlement since ancient times, evidence of an Iron Age coastal fort can be seen among the cliffs and caves of ***Porth Island***, a detached outcrop which is connected to the mainland by an elegant suspended footbridge and which lies to the northeast of the centre of this popular seaside and surfing resort. In common with many Cornish coastal communities, Newquay was an important pilchard fishing centre in the centuries leading up to the industry's decline early in the 20th century. An original *'huer's'* hut can still be seen on the headland to the west of the harbour; this was where a local man would keep a look-out for shoals of red pilchards and alert the fishing crews when one was sighted close to shore by calling *'hevva'* through a long loud-hailer. He would then guide the *seine* boats towards their quarry with semaphore-style signals using a pair of bats known as *'bushes'*.

The town takes its name from the new harbour which was built in the 1830's by Joseph Treffry of Fowey for exporting china clay, a trade which continued for several decades until the purpose-built port facility was completed on the south coast at Par. The decline of Newquay as a port was tempered by the arrival of the railway in 1875, and before long train-loads of visitors were arriving to enjoy the town's extensive sandy beaches, scenic position and mild climate. Today Newquay is one of Cornwall's most popular and liveliest resorts. Over the years, a number of popular attractions have been constructed to satisfy tourist demand, including ***Trenance Leisure Park*** with its boating lake and miniature railway. ***Newquay Zoo*** is also in the park, and features a range of environments and habitats for the resident wildlife, including an African Plains enclosure and Tropical House. The ***Sea Life Centre*** is another of the town's interesting attractions, and ***Tunnels Through Time*** brings to life stories of bygone days in Cornwall's past, with over 70 life-size figures.

Towan Beach is one of a succession of fine beaches overlooked by the town, a good sheltered beach with a tidal paddling pool which is ideal for children, which can be found at the base of Porth Island. In recent decades Newquay has also acquired a reputation as one of

Newquay Beach

the finest surfing centres in the British Isles. Throughout the year, thousands of keen surfers arrive in camper vans and the like to catch the waves of ***Fistral Beach***, or to watch the increasing number of national and international surfing competitions held here each season. Along with the cafes and giftshops, the streets of the town are lined with a refreshing variety of shops offering everything for the surfer, both for sale or hire. Another colourful summer attraction involves Newquay's fleet of traditional pilot gigs, 30 foot rowing boats which race each other over a six-mile course in the bay.

Roanne's Restaurant is a charming and welcoming licensed restaurant tucked away up a hill off the high street in Newquay. This homely and cheerful establishment offers an impressive range of tempting snacks and home-cooked meals including steaks, roast dinners, pies, fish, burgers, jacket potatoes and toasted sandwiches as well as curries and pasta dishes. There are also several vegetarian dishes and daily specials. Friendly and gregarious owners Darren and Jill Fortune make every effort to ensure visi-

Roanne's Restaurant

tors are made to feel welcome and at home. There is also bed and breakfast accommodation available here: the two large and comfortable family rooms above the restaurant are ideal for anyone wanting to stay in the centre but quiet enough to be out of the way of the usual hub-bub of summer life in Newquay. *Roanne's Restaurant, 5 Cheltenham Place, Newquay, Cornwall TR7 1BA Tel: 01637 874994.*

Overlooking the Barrowfields right on the coast, ***Kilbirnie Hotel*** is an elegant establishment offering comfort, excellent service and the highest standards of accommodation and cuisine. The tasteful and welcoming guest rooms, lounge and restaurant provide splendid comforts within a peaceful and relaxing ambience.

Kilbirnie Hotel

The distinguished menu features a superb choice of traditional English dishes, making the best use of fresh local seafood, locally supplied fresh vegetables and superior dairy produce. Pre-dinner drinks can be enjoyed in the bar and ballroom; there is live entertainment nightly during the high season. All this and a choice of excellent leisure facilities - including indoor and outdoor heated swimming pools, solariaum and sauna - make any stay at the Kilbirnie a luxurious experience. *Kilbirnie Hotel, Narrowcliff, Newquay, Cornwall TR7 2RS Tel: 01637 850769 Fax: 01637 850769.*

Around Newquay

Holywell Bay *Map 4 ref I8*

2 miles SW of Newquay off the A3075

Holywell Leisure Park and an attractive beach with towering sand dunes make this a popular - though not too crowded or busy - resort and tourist centre.

St Pirans Inn is a handsome restaurant and pub in Holywell Bay. The newly refurbished large wood-panelled bar area features open stone fireplaces and walls adorned with brass and bric-a-brac; the exposed beams in the bar boast regimental crests. The larger

St Pirans Inn

lounge/dining area is comfortable and welcoming, with an open slate fireplace. The menu features all local fish and produce and a large range of traditional meals. Real ales include those from local brewers as well as guest beers. Good walking is at hand and, should you choose to prolong your stay, the Inn has two self-catering flats available all year round. *St Pirans Inn, Holywell Bay, Newquay, Cornwall TR8 5PP Tel: 01637 830205.*

St Columb Minor *Map 4 ref J8*

2 miles E of Newquay off the A3059

St Columb Minor adjoins Newquay to the east, and has an impressive church whose 15th century pinnacled tower rises to 115 feet.

Kestle Mill *Map 4 ref J8*

5 miles SE of Newquay off the A3058

The exceptionally attractive small Elizabethan manor house, ***Trerice***, lies hidden in the lanes two miles northwest of Kestle Mill.

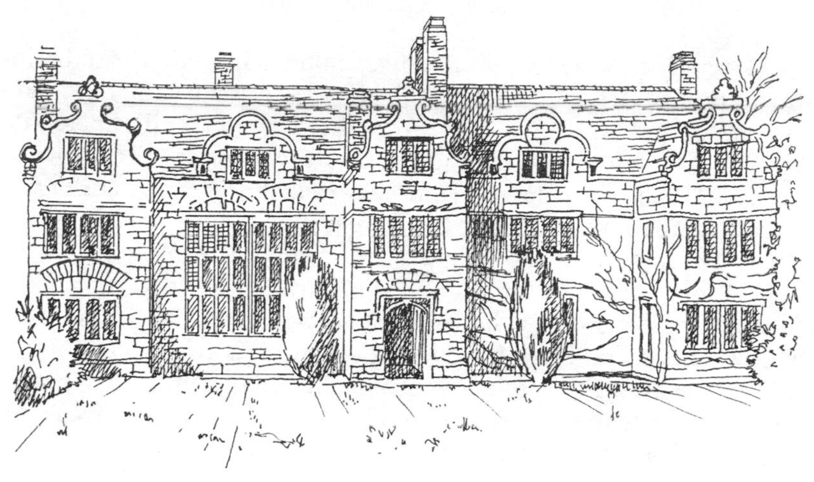

Trerice House

Built in 1571 on the site of a medieval predecessor, it was the family home of the influential Arundell family for several centuries. The structure has a characteristic E-shaped front and unusual carved gables, a possible Dutch influence, and stands within 14 acres of beautiful landscaped grounds. The interior is noted for its striking plasterwork ceilings, huge fireplaces and fine walnut furniture.

Most impressive is the great hall, with its delightful minstrels' gallery and remarkable window containing over 500 panes of glass, most of them original. An unusual small museum in one of the out-buildings is dedicated to the history of the lawnmower. The property is now under the ownership of the National Trust.

Newlyn East

Map 4 ref J9

6 miles SE of Newquay off the A3075

At Newlyn East the ***Lappa Valley narrow gauge steam railway*** carries visitors along an attractive section of the former GWR Newquay-to-Chacewater line. The short ride ends at a leisure park containing a number of historic attractions, including the imposing old engine house and chimney stack of ***East Wheal Rose***, Cornwall's richest lead-producing mine until a flash flood brought disaster in July 1846. Reopened the following year, it finally closed for good in 1885. Lying beside the A30 three miles to the east, ***Summercourt*** is worth a visit for its interesting country life museum.

St Agnes

Once known as the source of the finest tin in Cornwall, the old mining community of St Agnes lies at the head of a steep valley. Despite being subjected to 200 years of mineral extraction, and almost 100 years of tourism, it still manages to retain its original character, especially around the narrow-spired parish church and nearby terrace of stepped miners' cottages which are known locally as the *'Stippy-Stappy'*. The village is also renowned as the birthplace of the Georgian society painter, John Opie, and is known to thousands of readers of Winston Graham's Poldark novels as *'St Ann'*. A good local ***Museum*** can be found near the church, and there is also a popular ***Leisure Park*** to the south of the village which features a model of Cornwall in miniature and a number of themed areas, all set in seven acres of attractive landscaped grounds.

Trevaunance Cove near St Agnes is one of the best surfing beaches in Cornwall. A quay constructed here in the 18th century for loading tin ore survived here until it was washed away in a storm during the 1930s; its four predecessors having suffered a similar fate.

The Driftwood Spars is a handsome mid-17th century white-washed stone hotel and public house located in the superb sandy Trevaunance Cove on the edge of St Agnes - rugged Cornwall at its very best. Taking its name from the enormous ships' spars used in its construction, this welcoming establishment offers several bars and a ballroom/restaurant, all with a rich beamed interior, small

The Driftwood Spars Hotel

lead light windows and granite fireplaces. Each has its own character, though all share a welcoming, cosy ambience. Each of the guest bedrooms is unique, though all maintain a country cottage feel. Many offer breathtaking views and feature genuine Victorian half-tester canopied beds. In the bars there are six hand-pulled real ales, including a weekly guest beer on tap and, in the Lower Deck Bar, a collection of over 100 malt whiskies. The elegant restaurant upstairs offers an excellent menu which makes best use of the catch of the day and of the freshest local produce. *The Driftwood Spars Hotel and Freehouse, Trevaunance Cove, St Agnes, Cornwall TR5 0RT Tel: 01872 552428/553323 Fax: 01872 553701.*

From its clifftop position overlooking Trevaunance Cove with its lost harbour and sandy beach, ***Trevaunance Point Hotel*** on the edge of St Agnes offers magnificent cliff scenery from the comfort and elegance of a first-class hotel. The atmosphere within speaks of history and comfort, with its beamed bar and very attractive restaurant. Some guest bedrooms feature stone fireplaces, antique furnishings, marble washstands and other accoutrements which hearken back to more gracious days. Marc Watts has run the hotel

Trevaunance Point Hotel

for 23 years, ably supported by his wife Debbie, daughter Katie, and their efficient and welcoming staff. There is a hair, health and beauty salon, as well as the Porthole, a gifts department with a range of local products to be purchased. The hotel has a well deserved reputation for food ranging from the ample breakfasts, lunchtime lifesavers or the romantic candlelit evening meals. The restaurant has a reputation for fish and seafood dishes although meat and vegetarian selections are always available. The varied menu is complemented by an extensive wine list. To reach this marvellous establishment, drop down to the cove from St Agnes and follow the private road from the beach to its end. *Trevaunance Point Hotel, Trevaunance Cove, St Agnes, Cornwall TR5 0RZ Tel: 01872 553235 Fax: 01872 553874.*

The surrounding landscape is littered with abandoned pump houses and mine shafts (walkers should keep to the paths): many of the mines, such as Wheal Kitty and Wheal Ellen, were named after female members of the mine-owning families, or, in the case of Wheal Freedom and Wheal Friendly, were given other romantic associations. One of the most photogenic of Cornwall's derelict pump houses stands on a narrow cliff platform 200 feet above ***Chapel Porth***, a mile and a half west of St Agnes. Now under the ownership of the National Trust, Wheal Coates was in operation for 30 years between 1860 and 1890. A good circular walk from the car park at Chapel Porth also takes in St Agnes Head and St Agnes Beacon, a 628 foot peak which offers outstanding views across Cornwall to Bodmin Moor in the east and St Ives in the west; it is said that over 30 church towers can be seen from here on a clear day.

Around St Agnes

Porthtowan — *Map 4 ref H10*

1 mile SW of St Agnes off the A30

This typically Cornish cove, set in cliffs, has a good beach and is popular with surfers. ***Woodlands Restaurant*** is located in a secluded spot behind dense shrubbery, and is thus hidden away during the spring, summer and autumn months. This position is explained by a popular local myth featuring a fire-eating dragon linked with the Ghost of Cornwall. Hospitable, welcoming owners Neil and Amanda MacDonald will be more than happy to relate this tale to interested visitors. Set in three acres of grounds, this impressive mid-19th century restaurant boasts charming lawns and a southerly aspect, with views across open fields to Mount Ambrose. The main dining room comprises a large draped conservatory extending out onto the Mediterranean-style patio. From this large room guests enter the supremely comfortable lounge for a relaxing drink. There is also a darkened, intimate snug with a well-stocked bar, and a

Woodlands Restaurant

smaller inner dining room. The handsome, tasteful decor throughout enhances the warm and comfortable ambience. The extensive wine list offers whites, reds and champagnes from a dozen of the finest wine-producing countries. The tempting menu makes ample and excellent use of the finest local produce, enhanced by the subtle use of herbs home-grown by Amanda and Neil. *Woodlands Restaurant, Mile Hill, Porthtowan, Cornwall TR4 8TY Tel: 01209 890342.*

Bolingey

Map 4 ref I9

2 miles NE of St Agnes off the B3284

The Bolingey Inn is a welcome haven from the busy tourist and holiday spots nearby. Just one mile inland, visitors can leave behind the summertime bustle and wintertime sleepiness of the coast for the warm and welcoming Bolingey. Surrounded by public bridleways, an angling lake, bridge-crossed stream and handsome thatched cottages, this delightful countryside establishment is set back from the lane, with its own outdoor terrace.

The list of landlords goes back to1780 - guests can peruse this historic list if they wish - but the building is older than this. The country style furnishings in the main bar are comfortable and snug; there's also a smaller bar and a dining room, all crowned by a beamed planked ceiling. The low beams have their own story to tell, which convivial landlord Nick Page will be happy to relate. The home-made food and Sunday lunches, created under the careful eye of the chef, an ex-army cook, include such favourites as cottage pie, steaks,

The Bolingey Inn

chilli, seafood and others that live up to the highest standards of this great village pub. *Bolingey Inn, Penwartha Road, Bolingey, Perranporth, Cornwall TR6 0DH Tel: 01872 572794.*

Perranporth

Map 4 ref I9

3 miles NE of St Agnes off the B3285

This popular summer holiday centre lies on the coast. Formerly a mining community, all signs of its industrial heritage have long since disappeared, either as a result of encroaching sand or encroaching tourist development. The resort's main asset is its three-mile beach, a beautiful stretch of golden sand which is popular with bathers and surfers, although respect should be given to the inshore currents, which at certain stages of the tide can be hazardous. Winston Graham wrote his first Poldark novel here. Perranporth hosts a Celtic music and dance festival every October.

Perranzabuloe

Map 4 ref I9

5 miles NE of St Agnes off the A3075

Perranzabuloe means *'St Piran in the sand'* - for it is here that the 6th century missionary saint, St Piran, is reputed to have landed, having sailed from Ireland *'on a millstone'*. His landing place on ***Penhale Sands*** is marked by a tall granite cross, which is one of only two three-holed Celtic crosses in the county. St Piran, patron saint of tinners, founded a church and oratory half a mile inland, but by the 11th century it was entirely engulfed in sand, where it lay undisturbed until the 19th century. Now protected by a concrete shell, the delightful little building is worth making the effort to find.

According to local legend, the old mining town of Langarroc lies buried beneath the dunes of Penhale Sands. An ungodly community, it was swallowed up in a great tempest which lasted three days and nights as an act of retribution from on high. On stormy nights, it is said that ghostly cries for help can still be heard above the sound of the wind and waves. A remarkable carved Celtic face which once adorned St Piran's oratory has been remounted in the south porch of the parish church. Goonhavern's ***World in Miniature*** is also nearby.

CHAPTER FOUR
Mid-Cornwall South

Charlestown Harbour

Chapter 4 - Area Covered

For precise location of places please refer to the colour maps found at the rear of the book.

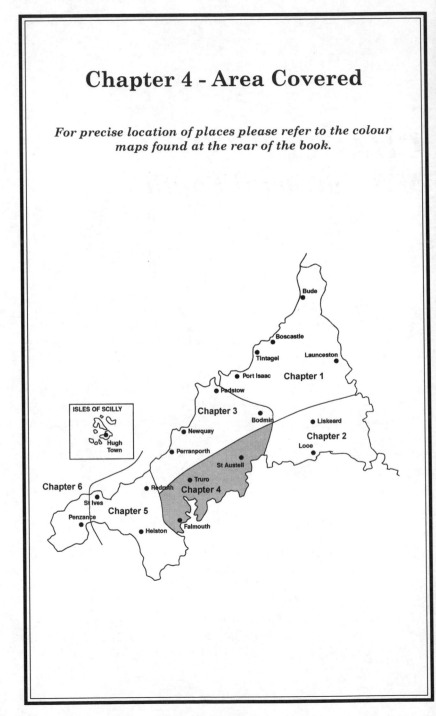

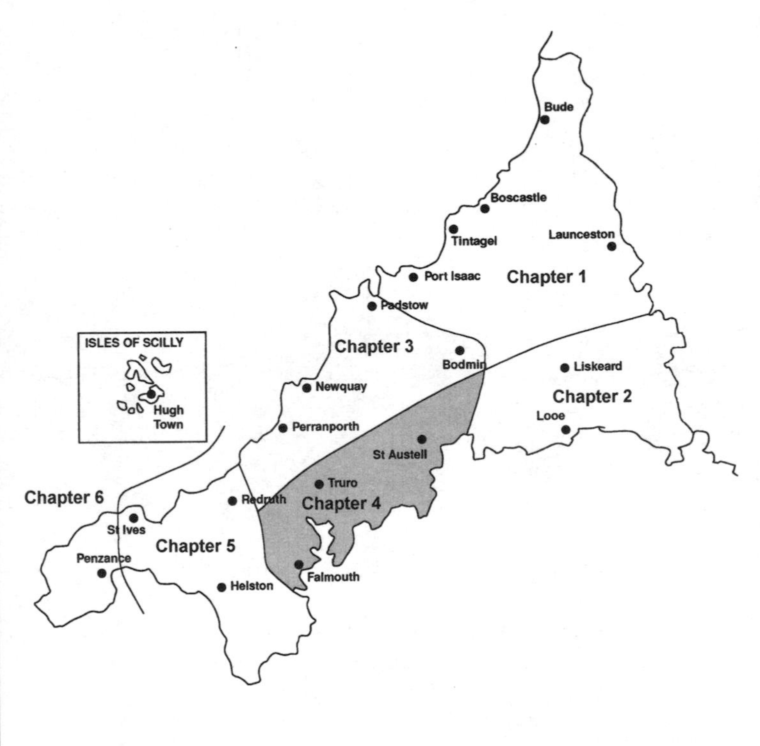

4
Mid-Cornwall South

Introduction

St Austell, Mevagissey, Truro - romantic associations abound when one thinks of this part of Cornwall. Still one of the world's largest producers of china clay - a surprisingly versatile material which, as well as being the basic ingredient of porcelain is used in the manufacture of paper, paint and pharmaceuticals - this region offers rugged coastlines, the beautiful towns and villages of the Fal Estuary (including, of course, the leading resort of Falmouth itself), and some exceptionally pretty coastal communities. The ***Carrick Roads***, a spectacular deep-water anchorage which is formed by the merging of seven river estuaries, is one of the many scenic highlights of the region, as is the famed ***Roseland Peninsula***, the name given the indented tongue of land which forms the eastern margin of the Fal Estuary.

This is a region of stunning gardens, including the famed Lost Gardens of Heligan, Trelissick Gardens, Carwinion, Glendurgan, and Trebah, each with its own horticultural history and wonders. There are also many stately homes in the area, such as Bosvigo House in Truro, Arwenick House in Falmouth, and the marvellous Pendennis Castle.

The legacy of Cornwall's seafaring heritage - of shipwrecks, booty and trawling - is also of course in abundance, in the shape of the many peaceful and secluded fishing villages that still exist.

St Austell

This sprawling former market and mining town was transformed in the second half of the 18th century when William Cookworthy discovered large deposits of china clay, or *kaolin*, here in 1755. Over the years, waste material from the clay pits has been piled into great conical spoil heaps which dominate the landscape to the north and west of the town. These bare bleached uplands are sometimes referred to as the *'Cornish Alps'*, although in recent years steps have been taken to landscape their surface and seed them with grass.

The narrow streets of old St Austell create an atmosphere more befitting a market town than a mining community. The central thoroughfares radiate from the parish church of the ***Holy Trinity***, an imposing structure with a tall 15th century tower which is decorated on all four sides with carved figures and topped by impressive pinnacles and crenelations. The granite facing stones were brought from the famous Pentewan quarries three miles to the south. The church interior has a fine wagon roof and some interesting early features, including a rare pillar piscina and a Norman font carved with a curious assortment of human heads and mythical creatures.

Elsewhere in the town centre there are some notable old buildings, including the ***Town Hall***, ***Quaker Meeting House*** and White Hart Hotel, as well as a good modern shopping precinct. Nearby, there's the ***Mid-Cornwall Craft Centre*** (at Biscovey), and the ***Automobilia Motor Museum*** at St Stephen.

Around St Austell

Boscoppa *Map 2 ref L9*

1½ miles E of St Austell off the A390

Tregrehan, a superb woodland garden on the outskirts of this lovely village, is well worth a visit.

Charlestown *Map 2 ref L9*

1½ miles SE of St Austell off the A390

Charlestown Harbour is a familiar location for TV programmes such as *Poldark* and the *Onedin Line*. Built in 1790 for the import of coal and export of china clay, this wonderful centre remains a Georgian time capsule, now providing permanent berth for square-riggers. The outstanding ***Shipwreck and Heritage Centre*** offers visitors a fascinating insight into the history of Chalestown and shipwrecks,

Charlestown Harbour

housing the largest general exhibition in the UK of artefacts recovered by divers. Animated scenes of village life, hundreds of photographs and prints, and the recovered valuables themselves - pewter plates, candlesticks, weapons, beads, gold and silver, among many others - make for a fascinating peek into the past.

Carlyon Bay

Map 2 ref L9

1 ½ miles SE of St Austell off the A390

Here on this marvellous inlet, Crinnis is a Blue Flag beach and neighbouring Polgaver is the only accredited naturist beach in Cornwall.

Carthew

Map 2 ref L9

2 miles N of St Austell off the B3374

Those interested in the history of the Cornish china clay industry should make for ***Wheal Martyn*** at Carthew. This fascinating open-air museum is set in an old clay works dating from around 1880, and features a giant restored water wheel, an exhibition of historic locomotives, and a unique collection of clothing and mining equipment used by local clay workers.

Bugle

Map 2 ref L8

4 miles N of St Austell off the A391

In common with the other mining communities throughout the country, there is a tradition for those in Cornwall to have their own silver band. Each year, the musicians come together to show off their skills and compete at the music festival here in the aptly-named village of Bugle.

The Bugle Inn is a welcoming and handsome stone-built former coaching inn standing at the main crossroads of this charming village. This pleasant pub epitomises a rural tin-mining hostelry, popular with locals and visitors alike. Away from the main tourist trails but still within close distance of Roche Rock, St Austell and other local attractions, the Bugle stands on the edge of a fascinating landscape of active and former china clay mining, reminiscent of

Bugle Inn

snow-covered alps and alpine passes. The interior of this early-19th century establishment features historical documents in display cases on the walls, along with an interesting bottle collection and carved relics, plush and cosy seating and stained timberwork. The food and drink on offer are excellent: St Austell ales and locally produced steaks and other home-cooked favourites such as sandwiches, salads and daily specials. Hosts Pam and Simon Rodger are also happy to provide two comfortable guest bedrooms should you wish to extend your stay in this delightful area. *Bugle Inn, 57 Fore Street, Bugle, Cornwall PL26 8PB Tel: 01726 850307.*

Roche *Map 2 ref L8*

5 miles NW of St Austell off the B3274

This old clay mining village (pronounced *Roach*) has a restored parish church which has retained its medieval tower and a pillared Norman font.

Even more impressive is the 14th century hermitage on ***Roche Rock***, the striking granite outcrop which stands beside the road to

Bugle half-a-mile west of the village. The feat of erecting this remarkable little two-storey building in such a precarious place is a testimony to the determination of its medieval builders. According to local legend, the hermitage was the cell and chapel of St Gonand, a saintly leper who survived thanks to his daughter, who each day carried food and water up the hill to her invalid father. The rock is also associated with the legendary Cornish scoundrel, Jan Tregeagle, who attempted to seek sanctuary in the chapel when being pursued across Bodmin Moor by a pack of headless hounds. Sadly, his torso became trapped in the window, exposing his lower body to the fury of his pursuers.

Pentewan

Map 2 ref L10

3 miles S of St Austell off the B3274

The east-facing shoreline to the south of St Austell shelters some exceptionally pretty coastal communities, including Pentewan (pronounced *Pen-Tuan*), a former quarrying village and china clay port which has found new life as a sailing and holiday centre. The enchanting ***Lost Gardens of Heligan*** can be found to the west of the B3273 between here and Mevagissey.

This superb 57 acre Victorian garden was restored after having been left to overgrow for over 70 years. Highlights include a subtropical valley containing the largest collection of tree ferns in Britain, an Italian Garden, Crystal grotto, and four walled gardens. The kitchen garden has been remodelled as a museum of 19th century horticulture, and there is also a pleasant sales area stocked with rare and unusual plants.

Occupying a truly superb location in 74 acres of unspoilt coastal farmland and enjoying breathtaking views stretching out over the bay and along the coast, literally a stone's throw from the sea, ***Polrudden Farm*** is a tranquil and welcoming retreat, offering ex-

Polrudden Farm

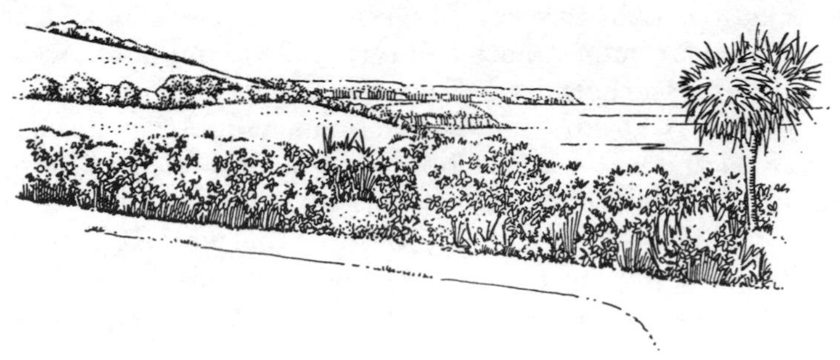

View from Polrudden Farm

cellent accommodation. It has its own small, secluded and private beach and is only five minutes' walk from Pentewan Sands, where you can enjoy safe bathing, water skiing, sailing and many other watersports. This small working farm is also handy for wonderful woodland walks, the National Trust coastal path, and the superb Lost Gardens of Heligan. There is a riverside cycle trail and a choice of three local golf courses. The comfortable and handsome guest bedrooms accommodate up to eight guests. The friendly, efficient staff make every effort to ensure that guests enjoy the best in hospitality and comfort. With all this and many fine restaurants and pubs nearby, Polrudden has all the ingredients for a wonderful break. *Polrudden Farm, Pentewan, Near Mevagissey, St Austell, Cornwall PL26 6BJ Tel: 01726 842051.*

Mevagissey

Once aptly known as Porthilly, Mevagissey was renamed in late medieval times after the Welsh and Irish saints Meva and Itha. The village is a renowned fishing port which was once an important centre of the pilchard industry. Each year during the 18th and 19th centuries, thousands of tons of this oily fish were landed here for salting, packing or processing into lamp oil. Some pilchards were exported to southern Europe, or supplied to the Royal Navy - to whose sailors they became known as *'Mevagissey Ducks'*. The need to process the catch within easy reach of the harbour created a labyrinth of buildings separated by steeply sloping alleyways, some of which were so narrow that the baskets of fish sometimes had to be carried on poles between people walking one behind the other.

Mevagissey Harbour

At one time up to 100 fishing luggers could be seen jostling for a berth in Mevagissey's picturesque harbour. Today, all but a handful of inshore fishing craft have gone and, in common with most of Cornwall's coastal communities, the local economy relies heavily on visitors, an annual influx which has given rise to a proliferation of cafes and gift shops, but which thankfully has failed to diminish the port's essential character. It remains the largest working fishing port in St Austell Bay.

The part-13th century Pentewan-stone ***Church of St Peter*** is worth a look for its Norman font and amusingly inscribed monument to Otwell Hill, an early in-comer who died here in 1617. Elsewhere, there are a number of more modern indoor attractions, including a ***World of Model Railways***, ***Aquarium***, and a ***Folk Museum*** containing an interesting assortment of fishing and agricultural equipment.

The Wheelhouse is located on the harbour front with magnificent views over the harbour and beyond to the fishing boats and leisure craft dotting the seascape. As befits a seaside establishment with a long tradition of service and excellence, boating memorabilia is a theme - lamps, oars, porthole-style windows - offering a welcoming, cosy atmosphere. The main restaurant, which is licensed, features an extensive menu including a selection of locally landed fish. In the upstairs restaurant the menu includes a good selection

The Wheelhouse Restaurant

of wines and spirits and a range of innovative fish, seafood, lamb, chicken and beef dishes. There are also four lovely guest bedrooms, all with harbour views, should you wish to prolong your stay in this delightful part of Cornwall. *The Wheelhouse Restaurant, West Quay, Mevagissey, Cornwall PL26 6UJ Tel/Fax: 01726 843404.*

Standing at the crest of a valley overlooking Mevagissey, ***Treleaven Farmhouse*** is a handsome and comfortably modernised establishment offering bed and breakfast, a distinguished restaurant and a wonderful base from which to explore the area's many sights and delights. Situated on the fringes of the Lost Gardens of Heligan and near beautiful coastal and country walks and many sandy coves, as well as the golf courses at Porthpean (3 miles' distant), St Austell (4 miles) and Carylon Bay (6 miles), boat hire, fishing trips, water sports and horse riding are all available just short drives away. Treleaven Farmhouse also has its own solar-heated outdoor pool, croquet lawn and putting green, as well as a games barn. Anne and Colin Hennah, owners of this working farm, offer guests a friendly and warm welcome. Cream teas or drinks from the bar can be enjoyed poolside; the extensive menu offers a superb range of delicious meals and snacks, many making use of

Treleaven Farmhouse

locally-raised produce. *Treleaven Farmhouse, Mevagissey, Cornwall PL26 6RZ Tel/Fax: 01726 842413.*

Around Mevagissey

Gorran Haven *Map 2 ref L10*

3 miles S of Mevagissey off the B3273

Once a pilchard-fishing community with a history to rival that of Mevagissey, Gorran Haven is now a pleasant village which has the added attraction of a sheltered pebbled beach. To the southeast, the land rises onto the impressive headland of ***Dodman Point***, much of which is owned by the National Trust. Sometimes known locally as *'Deadman Point'*, it is the site of a substantial Iron Age coastal fort whose 2,000 foot northern defensive earthwork can still be made out. The view northwest takes in the delightfully-named Porthluney Cove with its neo-Gothic flight of fancy, ***Caerhays Castle***, behind.

The ***Old Customs House*** is an attractive whitewashed cobb-built establishment dating back some three centuries. This licensed cafe offers a range of home-cooked meals for lunch and dinner, including locally-caught crab, sandwiches, snacks, salads, pasties, cream teas, cakes and a variety of speciality teas and other beverages, to be enjoyed indoors in this cosy and handsome cafe or outdoors when the weather is fine in the lovely and secluded walled garden. The charming and welcoming establishment is also home to a craft shop, which features locally produced crafts, paintings, jewellery, pottery, glassware, silver and pewterware, and a superb range of

The Old Customs House

gift ideas including dried flowers, baskets, windchimes and other attractive crafts and works of art. *The Old Customs House Craft and Licensed Coffee Shop, Gorran Haven, Near St Austell, Cornwall PL26 6JG Tel: 01726 843055.*

The Roseland Peninsula

This is the name given the indented tongue of land which forms the eastern margin of the Fal estuary, or ***Carrick Roads***. It can be approached along the coastal lanes or from the main A390 St Austell to Mevagissey road.

Grampound *Map 4 ref K10*

4 miles NW of Mevagissey off the A390

Although hard to imagine today, Grampound was once a busy port and market town at the lowest bridging point in the River Fal. A number of interesting old buildings are to be found here, including the guildhall, clock tower and toll house. The local tannery is renowned for its traditional methods of bark-tanning.

Creed *Map 4 ref K10*

4 miles NW of Mevagissey off the B3287

Just west of this charming small village, between here and Probus, is ***Trewithen House***, an elegant Georgian manor house built early in the 18th century by the Hawkins family, in whose hands it remains today. The exceptionally beautiful 25 acre gardens were planted by George Johnson, an authority on Asiatic flowering shrubs, and contain a world-renowned collection of magnolias, camellias, azaleas and rhododendrons which are particularly spectacular in late spring.

The grounds of Trewithen House in nearby Creed adjoin the ***Probus Demonstration Gardens and Rural Studies Centre***, a seven-and-a-half acre area of permanent gardens devoted to the study of plants grown in different soils and climatic conditions.

Probus — *Map 4 ref K9*

8 miles NW of Mevagissey off the A390

The village of Probus is famous for having the tallest parish church tower in the county. Built of granite in the early 16th century and towering to over 123 feet high, its three-tiered design, with its elaborate tracery, carving and pinnacles is an outstanding example of the *'Somerset style'*.

Tregony — *Map 4 ref K10*

6 miles W of Mevagissey off the A3078

Like Grampound, Tregony is a former river port with some fine old buildings, including a Gothic clock tower and a row of balconied almshouses.

Veryan — *Map 4 ref K11*

6 miles SW of Mevagissey off the A3078

Veryan is a charming village set in a wooded hollow which is famous for its five round houses. Set two at each end of the village and one in the middle, each of these curious whitewashed cottages has a conical thatched roof with a wood cross at the apex. They were built in the 19th century for the daughters of the local vicar, Jeremiah Trist. According to legend, their round shape is a defence against the Devil, who likes to enter a house by the north wall and hide in the corners. The much-altered and interesting village church is set above a delightful water garden which doubles as a garden of remembrance.

The ***art gallery*** is worth a visit, as is ***Caerhayes House***, designed by John Nash. The road to the safe sandy Pendower beach passes close to the Bronze Age round barrow on ***Carne Beacon***, one of the largest examples of its kind in Britain.

Truro

This elegant small city has grown to become the administrative capital of Cornwall. Its site at the head of a branch of the Fal estuary has been occupied for thousands of years, but it wasn't until large-scale mineral extraction began in medieval times that the settlement took on any significance. One of the first Cornish towns to be granted rites of Stannary, huge quantities of smelted tin or and other metals were brought here for weighing, taxing and shipping until the industry went into decline in the 17th century. By this time the estuary had also begun to silt up, allowing Falmouth to take over as the area's principal seaport. A number of picturesque alleyways or *opes* (pronounced *opps*) have survived from Truro's heyday as a port, many of which have colourful names such as Tippet's Backlet, Burton's Ope and Squeezeguts Alley.

In the historic centre of Truro, in the specialist quarter, you'll find ***Bazaar***, a unique shop tucked down an alley off Kenwyn Street. This distinctive shop features quality arts and crafts, produced by local and international artists and craftsmen. The staff are your knowledgeable and gregarious guides through the history, quality and provenance of wares - a fascinating array of artefacts and objets d'art, including furniture, pots, textiles and handcrafted gifts. This extravaganza of sights, aromas and sounds is the ideal place to find that unique present.*Bazaar, rear of 108c Kenwin Street, Truro, Cornwall TR1 3DJ Tel: 01872 242376*

Bazaar

In Little Castle Street itself you'll find ***Geneva***, which offers a superb collection of hand-made mirrors in a stunning array of colours and designs. Proprietor Robert O'Connell can also take

Geneva

commissions for mirrors made to your requirements. The shop also features individual and original picture frames, some painted on glass with a beaded relief which gives a stained-glass effect. Unusually there is also a choice of oval mirrors as well. Robert also offers a business card service: these unusual cards are works of art in themselves. The originality and craftsmanship of all the works on offer will please you; the very reasonable prices even more so. *Geneva, 2 Little Castle Street, Truro, Cornwall TR1 3DL Tel: 01872 277371 Fax: 01872 275578.*

Global Affair

Directly beneath the bell tower of Truro Cathedral, Cathedral Lane is another of Truro's specialist streets. This narrow mediaeval thoroughfare is home to a characterful collection of shops in listed buildings, offering a haven from busy traffic. Here you will find ***Global Affair***. This handsome shop houses a collection of craft items from around the world, as well as locally-produced pieces. This veritable Aladdin's Cave offers everything from African drums, Indian and Indonesian crafts, South American wall hangings, and bamboo, ceramic and metal mobiles to handmade and exquisite clothing from all parts of the globe, silver jewellery, carvings, sculptures, hand-printed textiles, throws, rugs and musical instruments. A true feast for the senses, this shop is a must for anyone interested in fine arts and crafts. *Global Affair, 7 Cathedral Lane, Truro, Cornwall TR1 2QS Tel: 01872 277023.*

An increase in metal prices during the 18th century led to a revival in Truro's fortunes; wealthy merchants and banks moved in, and the town became a centre for fashionable society with a reputation to rival Bath. This Georgian renaissance has left a distinctive mark on the town's architecture, particularly around ***Pydar Street***, with its handsome Assembly Room and Theatre, Walsingham Place, and ***Lemon Street***, one of the finest complete Georgian streets in the country. Also worth seeing are the indoor Pannier Market and the city hall in Boscawen Street.

At the edge of the main city centre on a bustling corner near the Law Courts, ***Oliver's Restaurant*** at the Wig & Pen pub offers excellent food and drink to its discerning clientele. This 18th century former Captain's residence is handsome and comfortable. Tucked beneath the Wig & Pen pub, a large, convivial public house apportioned into more intimate areas by exposed stonework, Oliver's is decorated in blues and yellows, giving it a comfortable, homely ambience. Caricatures of lawyers and judges, and historic photos of old Truro, adorn the walls. The menu is superb, making use as it does of only the freshest local ingredients. Fresh seafood is delivered daily; the produce comes from the market nearby. The changing menu -

Oliver's Restaurant

dependent on what is available and best (the chef is very particular about what he will accept) - will always include at least six succulent choices for each course, created and cooked in a style which adds innovation and tradition in equal measure. *Oliver's Restaurant, 1 Fromin Street, Truro, Cornwall TR1 3DP Tel: 01872 273028.*

A revival of the railway in 1859 confirmed Truro's status as a regional capital, and in 1877 it became a city in its own right when the diocese of Exeter was divided into two and Cornwall was granted its own bishop. Three years later, the foundation stone of Truro Cathedral, the first to be built in Britain since Wren's St Paul's, was laid by the future Edward VII, and over the next 30 years it was constructed to a design in Early English style by the architect John Loughborough Pearson. Finished locally-sourced granite and serpentine, this graceful three-spired structure incorporates the early 16th century south aisle of St Mary's church which originally occupied part of the site. The soaring 250 foot central spire can be seen for miles around and stands as a fitting centrepiece for this elegant and prosperous shopping and administrative centre. The ***Royal Cornwall Museum and Art Gallery*** is also worth a visit.

Those with an interest in gardening should make a point of finding ***Bosvigo House*** which lies just off the A390 Redruth road, three-quarters of a mile to the west of Truro city centre. This delightful series of walled herbaceous gardens is set around a handsome Georgian house (which is not open to the visitors); the grounds incorporate a woodland walk.

Around Truro

Ladock

Map 4 ref K9

5 miles NE of Truro off the A39

Set amid a colourful patchwork quilt of woodland, both deciduous and coniferous, and fields in a peaceful valley between Ladock, Mitchell, and Summercourt, just south of the main artery road through Cornwall, ***Arrallas*** is an imposing white-washed and stone-built Grade II listed farmhouse offering bed and breakfast in a tranquil and secluded location. Situated on part of theRoyal Duchy of Cornwall Estate, this distinguished country manor offers superb accommodations in its three elegant guest bedrooms, each of which is decorated to the highest standards of taste and comfort. The impressive, historic drawing room has a chaise longue, piano and other accoutrements that add to the country house feel. The generous farm-

Arrallas Bed & Breakfast

house breakfasts are served in the dining room, which looks out over a beautiful south-facing view. Owners Barbara and Ian Holt take pride in pampering their guests, offering a warm welcome and every attention to ensure that guests have a most enjoyable and relaxing stay. With excellent walking nearby, those interested in visiting this superior B&B are urged to phone for directions to this genteel haven. *Arrallas, Ladock, Truro, Cornwall TR2 4NP Tel: 01872 510379 Fax: 01872 510200.*

Come to Good *Map 4 ref J11*

3 miles S of Truro off the A39

In this delightfully named hamlet the road between Carnon Downs and the King Harry Ferry passes a pretty cob and thatch building which is one of the oldest ***Quaker Meeting Houses*** in the country. Built around 1710 when the Society of Friends was still outlawed, it is still in use to this day. Despite its pious-sounding name, the hamlet takes its name from the Cornish phrase *Cwm-ty-quite*, meaning *'house in the wooded combe'*.

A mile east, the National Trust-owned ***Trelissick Gardens*** lie on either side of the B3289 as the road descends to the King Harry Ferry. These beautiful wooded gardens were laid out in their present form by the Copelands between 1937 and 1955 in the grounds of a 19th century neoclassical mansion (which is not open to visitors). Renowned for their collections of mature trees and flowering shrubs, which include magnolias, rhododendrons, azaleas and hydrangeas, the gardens are particularly lovely in early summer. Special features include a summer house with a Saxon cross and a Victorian water tower with a steep conical roof and *'squirrel'* weather vane. A network of delightful woodland walks leads down to the banks of the Carrick Roads.

Feock

Map 4 ref J11

4 miles S of Truro off the B3289

This charming collection of whitewashed thatched cottages and affluent modern homes overlooks the deep-water estuary. The yew-filled churchyard contains a free-standing 13th century tower and is entered through an unusual lychgate incorporating an upper storey hung with slates. A pleasant creekside walk to the west follows the course of an old tramway, a sign that this tranquil place once had a bustling industrial economy. A land to the south of Feock leads to the tip of ***Restronguet Point***, the landing stage for a passenger ferry which once formed part of the main post route from Falmouth to Truro and beyond. One the southern side, there is an attractive inn, the Pandora, named after the ship which was sent out to capture the mutineers from the Bounty.

Mylor

Map 4 ref J11

5 miles S of Truro off the A39

Mylor and Mylor Bridge stand respectively at the mouth and head of a narrow arm of the Fal estuary. Once a small dockyard and landing place for the packet sailing ships which carried mail throughout the world, Mylor is now a popular yachting centre. The beautifully sited churchyard contains the graves of many sea captains and shipwrights who were based in the parish, some of which have amusing inscriptions. The church has two Norman doorways and a 15th century south porch beside which stands a round-headed Celtic cross which, at over 10 feet, is one of the tallest in Cornwall. Dating from the 10th century, it was rediscovered in Victorian times after having been used for centuries to prop up the south wall of the church.

Albion House is a distinguished and impressive part-Tudor stonebuilt country farmhouse offering self-catering accommodation. The former stables have been lovingly converted into a cottage, *'Little Albion'*, with three double bedrooms, living room, dining annexe, kitchen and private paved courtyard. In addition there are two self-contained flats overlooking the garden; each has a twin-bedded room and a large sitting room. The large garden is perfect for picnics. There is also a grass tennis court which can be hired for a small fee. Here in Mylor, a designated area of outstanding natural beauty, there is a wealth of opportunities for sailing and exploring the secluded inlets with their beautiful scenery and abundant birdlife. The sandy beaches of the North Coast are only 20 minutes' drive away. There are also many golf courses nearby, and the esteemed sailing school at Mylor Yacht Harbour. Owners Mr and Mrs Polglase

Albion House

are happy to supply guests with organic vegetables and other produce. They also own two cottages at nearby Hicks Mill, Bissoe - *'Bryher'* and the Georgian cottage *'Little Chycoose'*. Each has three double bedrooms, a garden and a garage, and is located in good walking country. *Albion House, Mylor, Near Falmouth, Cornwall TR11 5SQ Tel: 01326 373607 Fax: 01326 377607.*

St Just in Roseland

Map 4 ref J11

6 miles SE of Truro off the B3289

This enchanting hamlet has an exquisite part-13th century church which lies in one of the most superb setting in the country. Concealed in a steep wooded tidal creek and entered through a lychgate which is level with the top of the church tower, the churchyard contains a wonderful collection of trees and shrubs, including semi-tropical species such as the African fire bush and Chilean myrtle. Sadly, the church interior suffered a clumsy Victorian *'restoration'*, although the 15th century font and 16th century monumental brass survive. In 1733, a wealthy parishioner bequeathed 10 shillings (50 pence) a year to the vicar for dedicating a funeral sermon to him every 27th December.

St Just in Roseland

Portscatho *Map 4 ref J11*

7 miles SE of Truro off the A3078

This pleasant, secluded Roseland village and beach on Gerrans Bay is well worth a visit. Location for the TV drama The Camomile Lawn, it is also home to***Tregerein Guest House***, a truly delightful and welcoming B&B. Originally built for an old sea captain and recently renovated and extended to include a large, airy conservatory, the interior of this handsome Edwardian property boasts high (12 foot) ceilings and many original features. The attractive terraced garden overlooks the sea. Friendly, hospitable owners Stuart and Marianne Evans make every effort to ensure guests have a comfortable and memorable stay - Tregerein is popular with walkers and car tour-

Tregerein Guest House

ers, enjoying the panoramic views of Gerrans Bay and the adjacent coastal path. There are six spacious and tastefully furnished bedrooms. For classic car buffs the garage holds hidden treasure: Stuart collects and races vintage motorcars, and has won at Silverstone. Marianne is a keen horsewoman and will happily share information on good riding in the area. There is a choice of breakfast menus; packed lunches and evening meals are also available on request. All the food is home-cooked and home-prepared, using fresh, locally available produce. *Open all year. Tregerein Guest House, New Road, Portscatho, Cornwall TR2 5HD Tel: 01872 580336.*

St Mawes *Map 4 ref J11*

9 miles SE of Truro off the A3078

The popular yachting centre of St Mawes guards the eastern entrance to the Fal estuary. The town is dominated by its artillery fort, also known as ***St Mawes Castle***, which, along with ***Pendennis Castle*** on the western bank, was constructed in the 1540's as part of Henry VIII's coastal defences. Built to a characteristic cloverleaf, or trefoil, design around a circular central tower, its cannons were able to fire in a wide arc from a number of levels. Yet it was destined never to fire a shot in anger, and today its gun emplacements and restored Tudor interior remain in remarkably fine condition. The fort is surrounded by extensive gardens which offer dramatic views of Falmouth Harbour.

Dating back to the 17th century, ***The Old Watch House*** is a licensed restaurant with an intriguing history. This former Customs House, from which gigs would be sent to chase smugglers, features the original black-beamed ceilings and is decorated with seascapes, brasses, sea lamps, ships' ropes and other sea-faring memorabilia. The extensive and innovative menus (one for the hours between 10.30 and 6 p.m., and an a la carte and supper menu for evening meals) offer a tempting variety of traditional favourites such as steaks, seafood and a range of pasties for daytime meals, and imaginative dishes such as poached salmon and chicken St Lucia, as well

The Old Watch House

as delicious vegetarian options, for the evening menus. The wonderful desserts are home-made. The ambience in the comfortable dining room is relaxed and relaxing; the service is superb. Visitors return again and again to sample the delights of this charming and distinctive establishment. *The Old Watch House, No. 1 The Square, St Mawes, Truro, Cornwall TR2 5DG Tel: 01326 270279.*

Between the harbour and the castle here in St Mawes, ***Waterside Gallery*** is an attractive whitewashed establishment overlooking the estuary and the sea. The gallery features a wide range of works of art, including original paintings by local artists James Wood and Terry Bailey, who work in oils and watercolours and specialise in marine and landscape subjects. There is always a good selection to choose from, at a range of prices. The shop also features the work of other gifted local artists: there is an imaginative and artistic selection of woodturning crafted by Tim Spencer, hand-carved birds by Mike Wood, magnificent blown glass by Norman Stuart Clark, enchanting ceramics by Sue Reddington and Shirley Foote, and a wide variety of framed prints and cards. The gallery is run by the family of the artists, and visitors, whether browsing or looking to buy, are made most welcome. *Waterside Gallery, Marine Parade, St Mawes, Nr Truro TR2 5DW Tel: 01326 270136.*

The Waterside Gallery

Falmouth

Falmouth stands in a magnificent position at the entrance to the ***Carrick Roads***, a spectacular deep-water anchorage which is formed by the merging of seven river estuaries. Although a settlement has existed here for many hundreds of years, it wasn't until the 17th century that the port was properly developed as a mail packet station which subsequently became the communications hub for the British Empire. During its heyday in the early 19th century, Falmouth was the base for almost 40 sailing ships which carried documents, personal effects and cargo to almost every corner of the globe. A few decades later, however, the introduction of steam-powered vessels heralded the end for Falmouth, and by the 1850's the packet service had moved to Southampton.

Three centuries before, Henry VIII built a pair of fortresses on either side of the estuary mouth to protect the strategically important deep-water anchorage from attack by forces loyal to the Catholic faith. (The Pope's disapproval of Henry's marital and religious extravagance was well known.) ***Pendennis Castle*** on the western side is superbly sited on a 200 foot promontory overlooking the entrance to Carrick Roads. Its low circular keep has immensely thick walls and stands within a 16 sided enclosure; the outer curtain wall was added during Elizabethan times in response to the threat of a second Spanish Armada. One of the last Royalist strongholds to fall during the English Civil War, Pendennis only succumbed to the Parliamentarians following a grim siege lasting five months. The castle remained in use as a coastal defence station until the end of the Second World War and is now under the ownership of English Heritage. The spectacular viewpoint of ***Pendennis Point*** is also the location of the Maritime Rescue Centre, the operational headquarters which was opened in 1981 to coordinate all search and rescue operations around the British coastline.

That Falmouth was developed as a port at all was due to Sir Walter Raleigh, a man whose early vision was later realised by the influential local buccaneering family, the Killgrews. A monument to the family erected in 1737 can be seen in Grove Place, a short distance from the remains of their once-splendid Tudor mansion, ***Arwenack House***. Falmouth's Royalist sympathies are demonstrated in the 17th century parish church which is dedicated to *'King Charles the Martyr'*; much altered, it retains its curious rectangular tower and arcades with Ionic plaster capitals. Elsewhere in the town there are some handsome early 19th century buildings, including the ***Falmouth Arts Centre*** in Church Street, which began life as a Quaker institute *'to promote the useful arts'*, the synagogue in Vernon Place, and the Custom House with its fine colonnaded facade. A curious chimney near the Custom House was used for burning contraband tobacco and is still referred to as the ***'King's Pipe'***. The area around Custom House Quay has been made into a conservation area, the centrepiece of which is the tall-funnelled steam tug, the St Denys. This fascinating little ship forms part of the ***Cornwall Maritime Museum***.

The Boathouse is a charming and eclectic pub boasting one of the best views of Falmouth from the outdoor seated decking area. Decorated with sails and rigging on the ceiling and featuring wooden floors, attractive wood panelling and a welcoming open fireplace, the atmosphere in this comfortable establishment is convivial and

The Boathouse

lively. Manager Ginny Fergus and her friendly, gregarious staff make every effort to ensure that guests feel welcome. The daily menu changes from week to week, and features home-prepared and home-cooked meals and snacks, available from 12 - 3 and 6 - 9 p.m. A range of real ales complements the delicious food. Live music Wednesdays, Thursdays and Sundays. *The Boathouse, Trevethan Hill, Falmouth, Cornwall TR11 2AG Tel: 01326 315425.*

Modern Falmouth has a dual role as a commercial port and holiday centre. The docks continue to be used by merchant shipping, and there is still an indigenous ship-repairing yard. However, these traditional activities are perhaps overshadowed by the town's increasing popularity as a yachting and tourist destination. Throughout the year, visitors arrive by land and sea to enjoy the mild climate, pleasant atmosphere and excellent facilities. For those keen to explore the upper reaches of the Carrick Roads by boat, a variety of pleasure trips depart from the Prince of Wales pier, as do the cross-estuary passenger ferries to St Mawes and Flushing. The tree-lined square known as the *'Moor'* can be found a short distance inland from the pier; on one side stands the town hall and art gallery, and on the other a steep flight of 111 steps known as Jacob's Ladder leads up to a Wesleyan chapel. An attractive sight throughout the summer months are the periodic races between Falmouth's old gaff-rigged working boats. These colourful competitions evolved from the traditional practice of racing out to newly-arrived sailing ships to tender for work. A number of these handsome working vessels, some of the last examples in the country still to operate under sail, are used for dredging oysters from the Helford estuary.

The Boslowick Inn is an imposing Tudor-style pub on the outskirts of Falmouth, about 1½ miles from the centre. Owners Jim and Helen Moffat are Members of the British Institute of Innkeeping, and have run this spacious and comfortable pub for the past five years. The inn boasts five separate lounges, a family room, function room and outdoor play area. The decor features exposed black beams

The Boslowick Inn

and warm wood panelling, enhancing the cosy and welcoming atmosphere. The Carvery offers superb food - including steaks, seafood, duck and roast leg of pork - and is very popular: booking is advisable. There is also a large selection of real ales on offer. *The Boslowick Inn, Prislow Lane (off Boslowick Road), Falmouth, Cornwall TR11 4PZ Tel: 01326 312010.*

'Penlee' is a three-bedroomed bungalow in Falmouth offering self-catering accommodation. Within easy distance of Falmouth Harbour and the fishing village of Flushing, this spacious and welcoming retreat is attractively decorated and offers every modern convenience. The accommodation comprises fully-equipped kitchen, dining room, lounge, laundry facilities (including washing machine, tumble dryer and ironing board), spacious bathroom with walk-in shower and second, separate WC. Prices include unlimited hot water 24 hours a day, as well as all heating and electricity.

'Penlee'

From one of the bedrooms guests can enjoy views of the splendid harbour, watching local crews race each other in Classic Working Boats with their colourful topsails. The paved patio is the perfect place to relax. The property also includes a garage. With many good pubs and restaurants in the area as well, this comfortable and inviting bungalow makes a marvellous base for exploring west Cornwall. *'Penlee', Creation Accommodation, 96 Market Street, Penryn, Cornwall TR10 8BH Tel: 01326 375055 Fax: 01326 375088 email: falmouth@encompasstravel.com*

A lane to the southwest of Falmouth leads past the little-known ***Penjerrick Gardens***, an attractive wild valley garden laid out by the Quaker Fox family which contains one of the largest magnolias in the country. Penjerrick is also famous for its hybrid rhododendrons, which were developed by the head gardener in the 19th century, and for its bamboos and tree ferns.

Around Falmouth

Maenporth, Near Falmouth *Map 4 ref I12*

1½ miles SW of Falmouth off the A394

Tregedna Farm Camping Park is a well-kept and extensive campsite located on a quiet, gently sloping south-facing site on a 100 acre farm, situated in a beautiful wooded valley just half a mile from the safe sandy beach at Maenporth. This family-run campsite has ample parking, flush toilets and free hot showers. The laundry room offers abundant free hot water and a spin dryer; other facilities include hair dryers and electric shaver points and hook-ups. The farm shop sells milk, eggs and other essentials, as well as homemade cakes and Cornish pasties made on the farm by the family owners. Offering wonderful views over the surrounding countryside, Tregedna is a peaceful, secluded and welcoming haven. Also just a few miles from Falmouth and its harbour, picturesque docks and charming quays, the campsite is the ideal base from which to explore southwest Cornwall. *Tregedna Farm Camping Park, Maenporth, Falmouth, Cornwall TR11 5HL Tel: 01326 250529.*

Tregedna Farm Camping Park

Mawnan Smith *Map 4 ref I12*

2 miles SW of Falmouth off the A394

Mawnan Smith is graced with three outstanding gardens: ***Carwinion***, a 10 acre subtropical valley garden by the Helford River; ***Glendurgan***, a secluded valley garden of great beauty leading down to the Helford estuary, created in the 1830's by Alfred Fox, and known for its magnificent tulip trees, magnolias, camellias, Giant's Stride and wonderful laurel maze; and ***Trebah***, a superb ravine garden with rare trees and many exotics.

Carwinion, is a comfortable and attractive house which offers three large double rooms and a self-catering annexe; the atmosphere is warm and welcoming, and every effort is made to ensure that guests feel at home. The tranquil surroundings comprise the valley garden which runs south towards the Helford River. This garden was created in the 17th century and covers about 10 acres; it is home to one of the premier collections of bamboos in the country. There are also majestic oaks and copper beeches, sub-tropical plants, ferns and spectacular Gunnera Manicata, Cryptomaria Japonica, Arthrotaxis and Dicksonia Antartica. Azaleas, camelias and rhododendrons abound. This superb garden is open every day from 10 - 5.30. *Carwinion, Mawnan Smith, Nr Falmouth, Cornwall TR11 5JA Tel: 01326 250258 Fax: 01326 250903.*

Carwinion

Durgan, Near Mawnan
Map 4 ref I12

3 miles SW of Falmouth off the A394

This National Trust-owned fishing hamlet at the southern end of the valley leading down to the Helford estuary is a gem which should not be missed.

St Anthony
Map 4 ref I12

4 miles SW of Falmouth off the A394

On the remote southern side of the Percuil estuary, the hamlet of St Anthony contains a small church which is rumoured to have been founded after the young Jesus Christ had sheltered here from a storm at sea with is uncle, Joseph of Arimathea. The remains of a monastery which once stood nearby have been incorporated into the 19th century Place manor house. A good way to reach the western side of the Fal is via the ***King Harry vehicle ferry***, which lies two and a half miles along the B3289 to the north of St Just.

The unusually deep water in the Percuil estuary here is often used as an anchorage by ageing seagoing vessels waiting to be recommissioned or broken up for scrap - an unexpected and spectacular sight.

Penryn
Map 4 ref I11

2 miles NW of Falmouth off the A394

Before Falmouth's rise to prominence in Tudor times, the controlling port at the mouth of the Carrick Roads was Penryn, a now-tranquil place lying at the head of Penryn creek. During medieval times, this was the home of Glasney College, an important collegiate church which survived until the Dissolution of the Monasteries in 1539. (All that remains of the church today is some small sections of pillar.) Nevertheless, Penryn remains a well-preserved historic port with many fine buildings and courtyards.

At one time, granite quarried in the parish was exported from Penryn docks for use in such projects as the Thames embankment and Singapore harbour. The availability of the stone has left the old town with a legacy of fine Tudor, Jacobean and Georgian buildings; attractively restored, the centre is a well-visited conservation area. An interesting museum of local history is housed in Penryn's town hall, formerly the parish gaol. The two well-stocked reservoirs lying to the southwest of Penryn are contained within the ***Argal and College Water Park***; excellent facilities for sailing and windsurfing can also be found a couple of miles further west on the much larger Stithians reservoir.

Waterfront Restaurant

Situated on Islington Wharf in Penryn, with beautiful views over the river from its elevated aspect on the first floor, the ***Waterfront Restaurant*** makes a feature of locally landed fish and seafood, including mussels, whitebait, coquilles St Jacques and calamares. The tempting menu also boasts steak, chicken, pasta and vegetarian dishes. This spacious, attractive, airy and stylish restaurant is decorated with sailing memorabilia; the tables and seating are of antique pine. The spectacular views enhance diners' enjoyment of the excellent menu. This welcoming establishment also boasts a fish shop on the ground floor. Owners Pepe and Caroline Valles and their efficient and friendly staff make every effort to ensure that guests have a relaxing and memorable dining experience. *Waterfront Restaurant, Islington Wharf, Penryn, Cornwall TR10 8AT Tel: 01326 378208.*

Flushing

Map 4 ref J11

4 miles N of Falmouth off the B3292

Flushing is another attractive yachting centre, built by settlers from the Low Countries in the 17th century - it owes its name to seamen from Vlissingen, Holland - and still retains a distinctive Dutch/Flemish appearance. The narrow streets have several fine Queen Anne houses, many of these the former homes of Packet captains. It is served by the ferry from Falmouth.

CHAPTER FIVE

Northwest Cornwall & The Lizard Peninsula

Tate Gallery, St Ives

Chapter 5 - Area Covered

For precise location of places please refer to the colour maps found at the rear of the book.

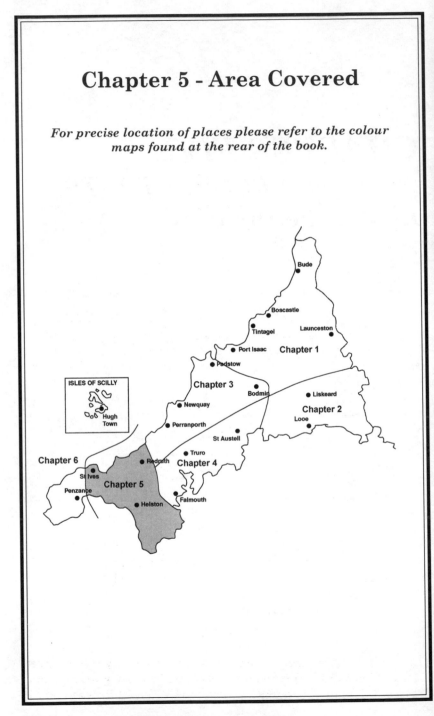

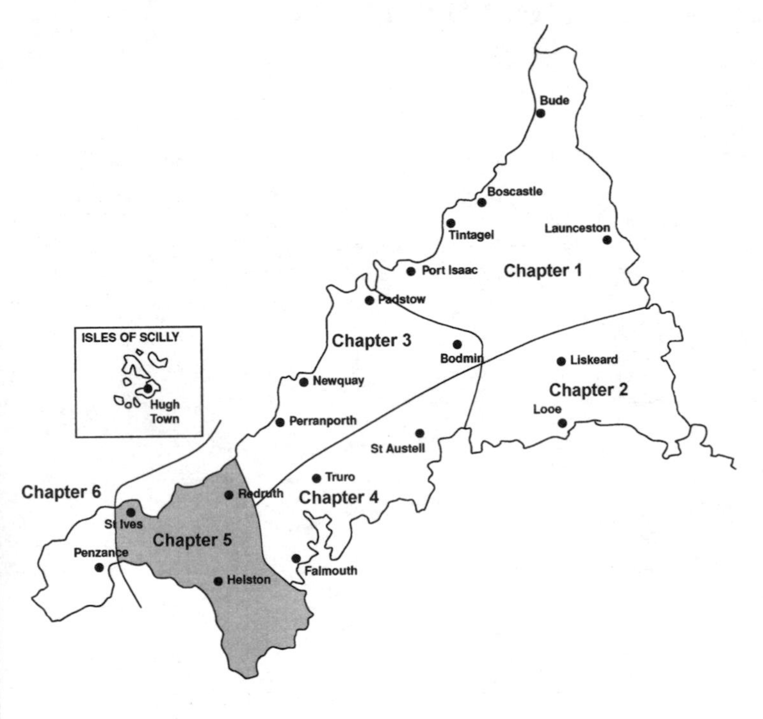

5
Northwest Cornwall & The Lizard Peninsula

Introduction

Northwest Cornwall has for the most part a mild climate with the help of the warm flowing waters of the Gulf Stream. Legends abound in the area, with tales of shipwrecks, smugglers and exotic sea creatures. Whilst fishing was always the mainstay of the local economy, the remains of the once-vital Cornish tin mining industry can still be seen, as can the great conical spoil heaps built out of the waste material from the china clay pits. The great beauty and isolation of this wonderful part of the county has been an inspiration to many artists over the years - St Ives became an artists colony for the likes of Whistler, Sickert, Nicholson and Lanyon, and continues to attract many painters and other artists today.

Today, tourists and visitors continue to flock to this part of Cornwall. The home of Britain's surfing fraternity, both the seacoast and the inland countryside have much to offer those who enjoy the outdoor life. The centres of Redruth, Helston and St Ives are characterised by their liveliness and beauty. Lizard Point, the southernmost point of mainland Britain, is dotted with exquisite fishing villages and breathtaking scenery.

Redruth

The southern approach to Redruth is dominated by the dramatic form of ***Carn Brea*** (pronounced Bray), a 738 foot granite prominence which is the site of the earliest known Neolithic settlement in southern Britain. The legendary home of a Cornish giant, many of the hill's features are dubbed with such names as Giant's hand, Giant's cradle, Giant's head, and even Giant's cups and saucers. (The last-named are natural rain-eroded hollows which over-imaginative Victorians thought had been made by bloodthirsty Druids.) The summit is crowned by an unprepossessing 90 foot monument dedicated to Francis Basset de Dunstanville, a benevolent Georgian mine- and landowner who did much to improve the lot of poor labourers. Much more attractive is the small castle on the lower eastern summit, a part-medieval building which in its time has been used as a hunting lodge and is now a restaurant. More easily approached from the south, the whole site is strewn with fascinating industrial and archeological remains.

Once the bustling centre of the Cornish mining industry, Redruth and the neighbouring ***Camborne*** have administratively combined to form the largest urban centre of population in the county. In the mid-19th century, the surrounding area was the most intensely mined in the world, and the district is still littered with evidence of this lost era. In the 1850's, Cornwall had well over 300 mines, which together produced two-thirds of the world's copper and employed around 50,000 workers. However, most had to close in the first few decades of the 20th century, when the discovery of extensive mineral deposits in the Americas, South Africa and Australia rendered the local industry no longer economically viable.

The National Trust's ***Norris Collection*** of minerals can be seen here in the geological museum of the old Camborne School of Mines Museum and Art Gallery. Still one of the foremost institutes of mining technology, the School moved to these new premises in Redruth in the 1970's.

The home of Scots inventor William Murdock, who settled in the area at ***Cross Street***, is open to the public. Murdock was responsible for such innovations as coal-gas lighting and the vacuum-powered tubes which were once a common feature in most department stores. Redruth also contains pockets of Victorian, Georgian and earlier buildings, particularly in ***Churchtown*** where there are some attractive old cottages, a Georgian church with a 15th century tower, and a lychgate whose unusually long coffin-rest was built to deal with the aftermath of mining disasters.

The B3300 to the northwest of Redruth leads past the ***Tolgus Tin Mill***, an 18th century streaming mill where tin deposits were extracted from the river bed by a process of sifting and stamping. Nearby, at ***Treskillard***, there is an interesting shire horse centre.

Around Redruth

Camborne *Map 1 ref H11*

1½ miles SW of Redruth off the A30

Along with Redruth, Camborne has much to offer those with an interest in industrial archeology. The home of pioneer Cornish engineer Richard Trevithick can be seen at ***Penponds*** on the southwestern outskirts of Camborne. This little-known inventor was responsible for developing the high-pressure steam engine, the screw propeller, and an early locomotive which predated Stephenson's Rocket by 12 years, yet he died penniless and was buried in an unmarked grave in Dartford, Kent. Known locally as the Cornish Giant, a statue of this underrated genius and accomplished amateur wrestler can be seen outside Camborne Library; he is also commemorated in the colourful Trevithick Day procession which is held in the last week of April. The ***Mineral Tramways Discovery Centre*** is also here.

Pool *Map 1 ref H11*

1 mile SW of Redruth off the A30

Midway between Redruth and Camborne, Pool is home to a pair of National Trust-owned massive old high-pressure ***beam engines***, one of which has a cylinder over 7 feet in diameter. One was built by Holmans of Camborne in 1887 as a winding engine for raising ore and delivering workers into the mine; the other was built by Harveys of Hayle in 1892 for pumping water from depths of up to 1,700 feet.

Busveal *Map 4 ref I10*

2 miles SE of Redruth off the A393

Near this scenic hamlet lies the mysterious ***Gwennap Pit***, a remarkable round grass-covered amphitheatre and former cock-pit thought to have been formed by the collapse of a subterranean mineshaft. Sometimes referred to as the *'Methodist cathedral'*, the founder of the nonconformist denomination, John Wesley, preached here on the first of many occasions in 1762. In 1806, seating terraces were cut into the banks, and the following year a Whit Monday service was established which has become an annual focus for Methodist pilgrimage from around the world. The nearby ***Museum of Cornish Methodism*** was opened in 1982.

Portreath *Map 1 ref H10*

2 miles N of Redruth off the B3300

Prior to a quay being constructed at Portreath in 1760, copper ore from the mines around Redruth and St Day had to be loaded onto ships from the beach, a slow and dangerous task. Built by Francis Basset, the man whose monument stands on Carn Brea, the harbour was connected to the mines in 1809 by the first railway in Cornwall. The remains of the inclined plane which was used to lower ore-laden wagons down the final 1-in-10 gradient to the quay can still be made out. The white conical structure on the cliff above the harbour was built in the 19th century as a daymark; known locally as the ***Pepperpot***, it continues to guide mariners to safety to this day. Now a pleasant and thriving small beach resort, modern housing now stands in the place of the great mounds of ore, coal and lime which once dominated Portreath harbour. The high headland to the west of the beach is known as the ***Wedding Cake***; it was once used by the local *'huer'* whose job it was to look out for shoals of pilchards and alert local fishermen. Much of the dramatic stretch of coastline to the southwest is owned by the National Trust. Portreath marks the start of ***Mineral Tramway Walks***, and ***Tehidy Country Park*** is close by.

Helston

Helston is the westernmost of Cornwall's five medieval Stannary towns. During the early Middle Ages, streamed tin was brought here for assaying and taxing before being despatched throughout southern Britain and continental Europe. Although difficult to imagine today, this was a very busy port up until the 13th century, when a shingle bar formed across the mouth of the River Cober, preventing access to the sea. Goods were then transported to a new quay at Gweek, until further silting and a decline in tin extraction brought an end to the trade.

Helston's long and colourful history has left it with a legacy of interesting old buildings. The ***Blue Anchor Inn***, a hostel for monks in the 15th century, can be found at the lower end of the main Coinagehall Street; further up, the part-16th century Angel Hotel is the former town house of the Godolphin family. In the 1750's, the Earl of Godolphin was responsible for rebuilding the parish ***Church of St Michael*** at the back of the town. It features an imposing exterior, fine plaster ceiling in the chancel, and impressive internal gallery on three sides of the nave. The church tower dates from the 1830's, its predecessor having been destroyed in a lightning storm almost a century earlier. The churchyard contains a memorial to Henry Trengrouse, the Helston man responsible for inventing the rocket-propelled safety line which saved so many lives around the British coast. Trengrouse devoted himself to developing the device after the frigate Anson ran aground on nearby ***Loe Bar*** in 1807, resulting in the unnecessary loss of 100 lives. An exhibit devoted to his life's work can be found in Helston's ***Folk Museum***, a fascinating collection of historical artefacts which is housed in the old Butter Market.

Helston continues to be a market town, and on Mondays the main thoroughfare is lined with colourful market stalls. The town's steeply-sloping streets contain a surprising assortment of Georgian, Regency and Victorian buildings, which together create a genteel atmosphere. In Coinagehall Street there is a fine neoclassical Guildhall, and in Wendron Street there's a modest thatched cottage that was birthplace to *'Battling'* Bob Fitzsimmons, who went on to become the world heavyweight boxing champion.

Helston is perhaps best known, however, for its ***'Furry Fair'***, which takes place each year on 8th May. This ancient pagan celebration takes its name from the Cornish word *fer*, meaning *'feast day'*, although in the 18th century it was renamed after the Roman goddess, Flora. According to local legend, what is now often referred to as the Floral Dance is performed in commemoration of St Michael's victory over the Devil, who tried to claim possession of the town. (The final boulder thrown by Satan, so they say, missed its target and ended up in the garden of the Angel Hotel, where it stayed until 1783.) Every 8th May the town is closed to traffic and formally-dressed couples and pairs of children dance through the streets, and in and out of people's houses, to the strains of traditional folk melodies.

When the shingle bar formed across the mouth of the River Cober in the 13th century, the dammed river created the largest natural freshwater lake in the county. Lying a couple of miles southwest of Helston and once forming part of an estate belonging to the Rogers family, ***Loe Pool*** is now under the ownership of the National Trust. A delightful six-mile walk leads around the wooded fringes of the lake, although those less inclined to walk the full distance can take a shorter stroll through the woods on the western side. This tranquil body of water is a haven for sea-birds and waterfowl, and is a paradise for ornithologists and picnickers.

A Cornish folk tale links Loe Pool with the Arthurian legend of the Lady of the Lake: like Bodmin Moor's Dozmary Pool, a hand is said to have risen from the depths to catch the dying King Arthur's sword, Excalibur. Another story connects Loe Bar with the legendary rogue Jan Tregeagle, who was set the task of weaving a rope from its sand as a punishment. A second monument to Henry Trengrouse, the inventor of the rocket-propelled safety line, can be seen on the cliff to the southeast of Loe Bar.

On the southern approaches to Helston, the A3083 passes close to ***Flambards***, a popular all-weather theme park set in attractive landscaped grounds and offering a variety of attractions, including an aero park, Victorian village, *'Britain in the Blitz'* exhibition and an assortment of up-to-date fairground rides. Penrose Estate is handy for lovely wooded walks.

Around Helston

Cury — *Map 4 ref H13*

3 miles S of Helston off the A3083

A number of stories abound about the small village of Cury which has an interesting church with a Norman south door. Apparently the *'Old Man of Cury'*, who rescued a stranded mermaid, was granted the power to comfort fellow mortals and break evil spells.

More probable is the story about a carter, who was driving a load of furze along the lanes when he realised it was on fire. As the flames leapt higher, he increased speed in a bid to reach a stream, increasing the airflow and making the situation worse. He released the terrified horses but the waggon and furze became a pile of smouldering cinders.

Colvennor Farmhouse is a part-17th century Grade II listed hotel and is approached up a long driveway. It is set within an acre of garden on the outskirts of the picturesque village of Cury, between Helston and Lizard Point. This handsome granite-fronted former farmhouse offers a welcoming and peaceful retreat. Owners Bob and Jackie Royds provide friendly service and warm hospitality in these most comfortable surroundings. The three double en suite bedrooms are furnished in traditional country cottage style; the ground-floor room overlooks part of the garden, while the two first-floor rooms offer far-reaching rural views. The guests' lounge has exposed beamed ceilings and is the perfect place to relax and pore over the wide selection of maps and books on hand to help with planning days out. Fresh local produce is used whenever available for the farmhouse breakfasts, served in the dining room, which overlooks the private front garden. The secluded coves of the Lizard peninsula are only two miles away and the locality is perfect for

Colvennor Farmhouse

walking, exploring and bird-watching. This attractive establishment also makes a wonderful base from which to explore southwest Cornwall. *Colvennor Farmhouse, Cury Cross Lanes, Helston, Cornwall TR12 7BJ Tel: 01326 241208.*

Nanplough Farm Country House is a true haven of peace and relaxation – the perfect place for guests to pamper themselves. This elegant establishment offers bed and breakfast accommodation. Guests will notice at once the grace and spaciousness of the house, though this in no way detracts from its homeliness and comfort. Built in 1887, it retains the grandeur of the Victorian age while being completely modern and luxuriously finished throughout. There are plenty of nooks where guests can curl up with a good book – the open fireside in the lounge is a favoured spot, looking out over the wooded valley with gentle pastures beyond. In the elegant dining room guests can enjoy the sumptuous breakfasts, and are also welcome to partake of the owner Jan's delicious home-prepared evening meals. All the rooms are spacious, lavish and feature large satellite TVs. The three on the first floor – the Gold, Blue and Burgundy rooms – afford impressive countryside views, while the ground-floor Rose Room is a cosy double room with every creature comfort.

As the name suggests, this B&B is located on a farm – 26 acres near the western edge of the wild and beautiful Lizard peninsula. Guests are welcome to stroll around the grounds – perhaps after a dip in the pool – or to follow the valley stream which flows down to

Nanplough Farm Country House

the excellent beach at Poldhu, a good starting point on the spectacular and exhilarating coastal path. Within easy distance, guests will also find Kynance Cove, Mullion and Coverack, the lovely Helford River and the breathtaking Lizard Point. There are also four self-catering cottages, part of the original farm. Clustered around a central courtyard, their innate character and history are revealed in their exposed beams and cottage-style furnishings and features. Sleeping between 2 and 6 persons, each has a patio and lawn. There's a children's play area and games room. Meals can be taken at the house if guests prefer, or *'al fresco'* at the poolside barbeque. For a truly relaxing and indulgent holiday, guests need look no further. *Nanplough Farm Country House, Whitecross, Cury, Helston, Cornwall TR12 7BQ Tel/Fax: 01326 241088*

Porthleven

Map 1 ref G12

4 miles SW of Helston off the B3304

This pleasant harbour town, developed in the 19th century, is still a working port, with a three-section harbour with wooden balulks that are lowered against storms. Located at the northern end of Loe Bar, Porthleven has a good beach, and the harbour accommodates a handful of fishing boats and a small boat-building yard. Its surprisingly substantial inner harbour was built in the middle of the 19th century, when there were ambitious plans to make Porthleven into a major tin-exporting centre. Although the scheme ended in failure, the inner basin can still be sealed off from the worst of the south-westerly gales, a periodic necessity in winter. A number of Porthleven's old industrial fixtures have been converted into handsome craft galleries and the like, and higher up the harbour is overlooked by an assortment of attractive residential terraces, fishermen's cottages, and inns. One street is named after Porthleven-born Guy Gibson, the instigator of the famous *'Dambusters'* bouncing bomb missions during the Second World War.

The Atlantic Inn sits above the gently sloping cliff road on the eastern side of this old fishing village. Porthleven once had a sizeable fishing industry, and was a major exporter of pilchard and other species of fish to the Mediterranean. The fishery collapsed in 1896 due to over-fishing and a significant part of the community was forced to emigrate to South Africa and the USA to find work, in either fishing or mining.

To reach this comfortable, yet unpretentious hostelry, follow the road around past the clock tower and up the hill turning left at the top. Here you can sit outside on the south-facing sun terrace, which is often bathed in glorious sunshine in summer, and enjoy the panorama of Mount's Bay stretching from Lizard Point to Gwennap Head. It is the perfect spot for a *'sundowner'* or a bite to eat at midday or early evening.

The Atlantic Inn

The inn is situated in a peaceful part of the village, away from the summer crowds. It has a relatively short tourist season and therefore largely relies on local trade for much of the year. This is reflected in the astonishingly low prices. Val and Roger, the owners, buy, prepare and cook the food themselves. They offer a sensible range of snacks and main meals which include rump steaks, home-made steak and kidney pies, half chickens, horseshoe gammon and fresh fish as well as vegetarian dishes. Roger's speciality is his curries – both meat and vegetable. All main dishes are uniquely priced at £4.95, explaining the number of *'locals'* that dine here regularly throughout the year. *The Atlantic Inn, Portleven, Cornwall TR13 9DZ Tel: 01326 562439*

Breage — *Map 1 ref G12*

4 miles W of Helston off the A394

Breage (pronounced *Braig*) is renowned for its exceptional 15th century parish church of ***St Breaca***. Large by Cornish standards, it has a soaring three-stage pinnacled tower and contains a remarkable set of medieval wall paintings which lay undiscovered under a layer of whitewash until the 1890's. The murals are as old as the church itself, and depict such subjects as St Christopher, and Christ Blessing the Trades. In the north aisle there is also a rare Roman milestone from the 3rd century AD, evidence that Cornish tin was extracted on behalf of the Roman Empire. The churchyard contains a Celtic four-holed wheel cross, the only example of its kind in Cornwall to be carved in sandstone, and affords a stunning view of Mount's Bay and the western side of the Lizard Peninsula.

Evidence of the area's industrial heritage can be seen to the southwest of Breage: the chimney and engine house of ***Wheal Prosper*** and the ruins of ***Wheal Trewavas*** both lie beside the coastal path on Trewavas Head.

Germoe — *Map 1 ref G12*

6 miles W of Helston off the A394

In the church in Germoe there is a remarkable Celtic font carved with a gaunt human head which is said to have come from the baptistery founded by the Irish king and missionary, *Germochus*, in the 6th century. There are good, safe sandy beaches at nearby ***Praa Sands***, and beyond ***Cudden Point***.

Prussia Cove is so-named for being the haunt of John Carter, a notorious 18th century smuggler who is rumoured to have modelled himself on Frederick the Great of Prussia. One story records how he used a cannon mounted on the cliff to scare off revenue cutters.

The smugglers' wheel tracks can still be seen in the steep stone slipway leading up from the water's edge.

Wendron *Map 1 ref H12*

4 miles NE of Helston off the B3297

One of the Romans' principal sources of tin ore was a mine near this handsome village. Re-dubbed ***Poldark Mine & Heritage Complex***, it offers visitors the opportunity to experience conditions in an underground mine at first hand. The three acre site incorporates a number of impressive above-ground visitor attractions, including a working beam-engine and an interesting collection of historic mining machinery and related artefacts. The mine lies within a popular fun park containing fairground rides, a cinema, picnic gardens and a variety of children's attractions. Letters posted in the unique underground postbox are stamped with a special postmark.

Sithney *Map 1 ref H12*

3 miles NW of Helston off the B3303

Parc-An-Ithan is a handsome guesthouse standing in its own grounds in the village of Sithney, convenient for exploring Land's End, the Lizard peninsula and other regions of southwest Cornwall. Proprietors Mark and Christine Channing extend a warm and friendly welcome to all their guests. The six attractive en suite bedrooms (including one with a marvellous four-poster bed) are spacious and very comfortable. Most enjoy panoramic views of the surrounding countryside. Meals are taken in the roomy dining room which is also open to non-residents. The Table d'Hote menu changes daily;

Parc-An-Ithan

there is also a full a la carte menu. Mark is also the chef; he brings over 10 years of experience to the excellent dishes he prepares, which make use of the freshest local ingredients.

The wine list and fully-stocked bar provide a range of beers and spirits. With all this and several sandy beaches within 10 minutes' drive, as well as spectacular coastal scenery and the golf courses at Praa and Mullion, guests are sure to enjoy their stay at Parc-An-Ithan, which also makes a very good base from which to explore this part of Cornwall. *Parc-An-Ithan, Sithney, Near Helston, Cornwall TR13 0RN Tel: 01326 572565.*

Godolphin Cross *Map 1 ref G12*

8 miles NW of Helston off the B3302

The exceptional part-Tudor ***Godolphin House***, featured in the Poldark series, can be found in the wooded lanes midway between this village and Townshend. Part early 16th century with substantial Elizabethan and Carolean additions, this is the former home of the Earls of Godolphin, prominent Cornish entrepreneurs who amassed a fortune from their mining interests.

The unique north front was completed shortly after the English Civil War and incorporates an impressive seven-bay granite colonnade. The interior is noted for its splendid King's Room, fine Jacobean fireplaces, and a painting of the famous *'Godolphin Arabian'*, a stallion imported by the second Earl which is said to be one of the three from which all British thoroughbred horses are descended.

There is some excellent walking on nearby ***Tregonning Hill***, a site littered with Bronze Age remains which also has an important place in industrial history, for it was here that William Cookworthy first discovered china clay, or kaolin, in the 1740's. An Admiralty signalling station was also established here during the Napoleonic Wars.

Culdrose *Map 4 ref H12*

1 miles S of Helston off the A3083

The ***Royal Naval Air Station*** at Culdrose is one of the largest and busiest helicopter bases in Europe. With a range incorporating several hundred miles of the British coastline and extending well out into the Atlantic, aircraft from here have been responsible for a great many successful search and rescue missions since the base was established in the 1940's. Visitors can observe the many comings and goings from a special public viewing area near the car park.

Gweek

Map 4 ref H12

3 miles SE of Helston off the B3293

Gweek stands at the head of the westernmost branch of the ***Helford River***. Although it is hard to imagine today, this was once a flourishing commercial port whose importance grew when the harbour at nearby Helston silted up in the 13th century. Gweek eventually suffered the same fate, and the cargo vessels of old have long since been replaced by small pleasure craft and sailing dinghies. In recent years, however, the port has undergone something of a rejuvenation with the opening of the ***Quay Maritime Centre***, the largest collection of historic small craft in Cornwall. Another of Gweek's attractions is the ***Cornish Seal Sanctuary***, which can be found a short distance from the village on the northern side of the creek. Injured seals and orphaned pups are brought here from all over the country for treatment and care before being returned to the wild; there is an underwater observatory which allows visitors to see the seals close to.

Just to the North of Gweek in the charming hamlet of ***Torvan Cross*** is the unusual location of a massive Bronze Age monolith known as the ***Tolvan Holed Stone***. In the back garden of a cottage and standing 7 feet tall, this curious triangular stone is said to bring fertility to those who squeeze their naked bodies through its 17 inch circular aperture.

Helford

Map 4 ref I12

7 miles W of Helston off the B3293

During the summer, a passenger ferry operates between Helford Passage and the village of Helford on the southern bank. This picture-postcard village stands in one of the most lush and attractive settings in Cornwall, the secluded tree-line estuary of the ***Helford River***. Once the haunt of smugglers, this deep series of tidal creeks is also rumoured to be the home of *Morgawr*, the legendary Helford monster. Since his first recorded sighting in 1926, he has been seen on a number of occasions and described as a *'hideous hump-backed creature with stumpy horns'*. The village itself has a charming, relaxed atmosphere, with traffic being banned from the streets during the summer months.

The ***Frenchman's Creek*** immortalised by Daphne du Maurier in her novel of the same name lies half a mile to the west of Helford village. Although best seen by boat, land access to this beautiful wooded inlet can be made via the farm at Kestle, which is signposted off the road to ***Manaccan***, another attractive village standing at the head of a tidal creek.

Mawgan

Map 4 ref H12

3½ miles SE of Helston off the B3293

Trelowarren House here in Mawgan is an impressive part-Tudor country mansion which has been the home of the Vyvyan family since the 15th century. Its main rooms and chapel are open to visitors on conducted guided tours.

The Old Court House is a handsome and traditional pub run by Sue and Louie Harris. Situated in the beautiful country village of Mawgan amid picturesque scenery, it was, as its name suggests, originally a local court house with a long and distinguished history. Sue and Louie have created a warm and appealing atmosphere. Sue

The Old Court House

does all the cooking and the menu offers a wide range of meals, using the freshest local ingredients and including monkfish, salmon, pasta dishes and steaks. There are real ales including IPA, Flowers, Pedigree and special guest beers. There is a tranquil beer garden situated away from the road and safe for children to play in. *The Old Court House, Mawgan, Helston, Cornwall TR12 6AD Tel: 01326 221240.*

Lizard Peninsula

The landscape changes dramatically to the south of Helford, from the luxuriance of the Helford River to the rugged splendour of the Lizard Peninsula. Here the land rises onto Goonhilly Downs, an area of windswept granite and serpentine heathland which is littered with Bronze Age remains and some rather more up-to-the-minute human creations - the huge saucer aerials and satellite dishes of British Telecom's ***Goonhilly Downs Earth Station***. Chosen for its location on solid bedrock near the most southerly point on the UK mainland, this important international telecommunications link can be seen beside the B3293 midway between Helston and the coast. A guided tour of the station can be taken during the summer months which incorporates an informative audiovisual presentation on the development of modern satellite communications.

As well as being of interest to the Bronze Age archeologist, the Lizard is of special interest to the botanist. The peninsula's moorland and cliffs are home to a number of rare wild plants, including the pink-flowering *'Cornish Heath'*, and a nature reserve has been established on ***Predannack Downs*** to preserve this valuable natural habitat. The rugged and undulating stretch of the ***South West Coast Path*** around the Lizard is among the most spectacular in Cornwall.

Lizard Point is the southernmost point on mainland Britain. Once the location of a coastal beacon, it was from here that the alarm was raised when the Spanish Armada was first sighted entering the western English Channel in 1588. The jagged fingers of serpentine and granite which project into the sea have long been a hazard for shipping, and as long ago as 1620, a lighthouse was erected on the headland to alert passing vessels of the danger. The original coal-fired warning light was erected by the notorious Killigrew family of Falmouth who were subsequently accused of trying to prevent shipwrecks on the Lizard so that vessels might founder nearer the Carrick Roads, where they held the appropriate rights of salvage. A more dependable lighthouse was established here in 1752, which was then taken over by ***Trinity House*** in 1790. Converted from coal to oil in 1815 and then to steam-driven electric power in 1878, it now has a tremendously powerful beam which can sometimes be seen from over 50 miles out at sea.

Lizard Village *Map 4 ref H14*

11 miles S of Helston on the A3083

This charming village just north of Lizard Point supplements its living producing ornaments crafted from local stone, and sold from the giftshops clustered around the village green.

The Caerthillian is an attractive bed and breakfast situated in the heart of The Lizard village, Cornwall's southernmost point. Owners Colin and Judith Hendy welcome guests to their Victorian home, providing a tranquil atmosphere in which to relax and unwind. The Lizard is famous for its beautiful coastal scenery; the constantly changing mood of the sea transforming the breathtaking views. Take

The Caerthillian

time to walk the Cornish coastal path, at its most magnificent around the tip of The Lizard Peninsula, or laze away the hours on The Lizard's unspoilt and secluded beaches. The village church, which dates back to 600 AD, is a haven of peace and beauty. Golf, sailing and fishing are within easy distance, as are wonderful gardens and memorable houses. The six guest rooms are comfortably furnished; some offer sea views. Judith prepares delicious meals using the finest local produce, including locally landed fish and seafood, to be complemented by fine wine from Colin's cellar: the perfect end to a perfect day. *The Caerthillian, The Lizard, Helston, Cornwall TR12 7NQ Tel/Fax: 01326 290019.*

Cadgwith *Map 4 ref I14*

1½ miles NE of Lizard Village off the A3083

This minuscule and very picturesque fishing village on the east coast of the Lizard Peninsula was once a thriving centre of the pilchard trade. It holds the record for the most pilchards caught in a single day: 1.3 million. There are two small shingle beaches and a cluster of pastel-washed thatched cottages.

Kynance Cove *Map 1 ref H14*

1 mile NW of Lizard Village off the A3083

The National Trust owns this famed beauty spot, which has a marvellous sandy beach and dramatic offshore rock formations.

Carleon Cove *Map 4 ref II13*

2 ½ miles N of Lizard Village off the A3083

The ruins of Poltesco serpentine stone factory here in this National Trust-owned village are worth a visit. Nearby is the popular beach at Kennack Sands.

Mullion Cove *Map 1 ref H13*

4 miles NW of Lizard Village off the B3296

Mullion Cove has a remarkable little weather-worn harbour. The view to the west of Lizard Point is enhanced by the sight of ***St Michael's Mount***, some 12 miles away across Mount's Bay. The interesting church has carved bench ends, and stands above the sturdy harbour of the National-Trust owned ***Porth Mellin***. There's some excellent walking in the area.

A mile north of Mullion, a memorial on the cliff above ***Poldhu Cove*** commemorates the work of Guglielmo Marconi, the radio pioneer who transmitted the first transatlantic wireless message from here in 1901. The previous year, Marconi had chosen this lonely spot to build one of the largest wireless stations the world had ever seen, a complicated affair of pylons and aerials which survived which survived until the 1930's. Marconi's achievement is commemorated by a small granite obelisk near the Poldhu Hotel, which was unveiled by his daughter after the inventor's death.

In 1785, a ship carrying a consignment of silver dollars ran aground on nearby ***Gunwalloe Church Cove***, a place which is still popular with treasure hunters, who can be seen combing the sandy beach with metal detectors. The charming little church which gives the cove its name lies protected in the sand dunes behind a cliff. Rebuilt in the 15th century on the site of an earlier structure, it is named after a little-known 6th century Breton abbot, St Winwalloe.

Coverack *Map 4 ref I13*

5 miles NE of Lizard Village off the B3294

This unspoiled fishing village has a minuscule quay and traditional cottages spilling down to the sea. It has been for many years an RNLI station, because of its proximity to the feared Manacles Reef.

St Keverne *Map 4 ref I13*

6 miles NE of Lizard Village off the B3293

This pleasant village has a handsome square. Four hundred shipwreck victims of nearby Manacles Reef are buried in the village churchyard. St Keverne was also the birthplace of two Cornish rebellions. There are good beaches nearby at Porthallow, Housel Bay and Kennack Sands, and nature trails from Tregallast Barton farm. Every August St Keverne hosts a celebratory Ox Roast.

St Ives

With its five sandy beaches, maze of narrow streets and picturesque harbour and headland, the attractive fishing and former mining centre of St Ives manages to retain a special atmosphere, despite being deluged with visitors throughout the summer. The settlement takes its name from the 6th century missionary saint, St Ia, who is said to have landed here having sailed across from Ireland on an ivy leaf. The 15th century ***parish church*** near the harbour's shorter west pier bears her name. An impressive building with a soaring pinnacled tower, it contains an unusual granite font carved with stylised angels and lions. Another striking ecclesiastical building, a mariner's chapel, stands on ***St Ives Head***, the promontory to the north of the harbour which is known locally as the *'Island'*.

The headland is also the location of a *'huer's'* hut, the viewpoint from which a local man would keep a look-out for shoals of pilchards in the bay. When one was sighted, he would alert the crews of the seine boats (open rowing boats) by calling *'hevva'* through a long loud-hailer, before guiding the fishermen towards their goal with semaphore-type signals using a pair of oval bats known as *'bushes'*.

St Ives was one of Cornwall's most important pilchard fishing centres until the industry went into decline early in the 20th cen-

St Ives

tury. The town holds a record dating back to 1868 for the greatest number of fish caught in a single seine net. Once the pilchards were brought ashore, they were compressed to release fish oil before being salted and packed into barrels for despatch to southern Europe, where the Catholic stricture regarding not eating meat on Fridays guaranteed a steady demand. On catch days the streets of St Ives would stream with the oily residue of these plentiful fish, and the air would be filled with an appalling smell which would drive away all but the most determined outsiders. A local speciality, *'heavy'*, or hevva cake, was traditionally made for the seiners on their return with their catch.

As well as providing shelter for the fishing fleet, St Ives' harbour was built for exporting locally-mined metal ores. The sturdy main pier was built by John Smeaton, the 18th century marine architect who was responsible for designing the famous Eddystone lighthouse which now stands on Plymouth Hoe.

Like many parts of western Cornwall, the surrounding valley was once rich in veins of tin, copper and other minerals, and indeed the building which now houses ***St Ives Museum*** began life as Wheal Dream copper mine. The town's labyrinth of narrow streets was once divided into two communities: *'Downalong'*, where the fishing families lived, and *'Upalong'*, which was inhabited by the mining community. There was much tension between the two, and fights would often break out between gangs of young rivals, a practice which ended with the closing of the mines and the steady reduction in the fishing fleet.

One of St Ives' most colourful inhabitants was John Knill, the 18th century mayor who was responsible for constructing the unusual steeple to the south of the town, supposedly as a mausoleum. Despite being a customs officer by profession, Knill was also widely rumoured to be an energetic smuggler who built the tall monument for the purpose of guiding vessels filled with contraband to the shore (it still serves as a mariners' daymark). He was actually buried in London, but bequeathed a sum to the citizens of St Ives for holding a curious ceremony which continues to be held in the town at five yearly intervals. On 25 July in the first and sixth years of the decade, a procession led by a fiddler, two widows and ten young women sets out from the centre to dance around the steeple and sing the old 100th Psalm.

St Ives' decline as a mining and fishing centre has been offset by its rise as an artists' colony. The painter William Turner visited the town towards the end of his life, and both Whistler and Sickert are known to have been attracted here by the special quality of the light in west Cornwall. In the first half of the 20th century, Barbara Hepworth, Ben Nicholson and others began to convert the disused pilchard cellars and sail lofts around the harbour into artists' studios, and a *'St Ives School'* was established which gained an international reputation. The town's artistic standing was also boosted by the arrival in the 1920's of the potter Bernard Leach, who established a workshop at ***Higher Stennack*** (beside the B3306) which is still in operation.

One of the highlights of any stay in St Ives is a visit to the ***Barbara Hepworth Sculpture Garden*** and Museum in Barnoon Hill. After she died in a fire on the premises in 1975, the sculptor's living quarters, studio and garden were turned into a museum and gallery dedicated to her life and work. The garden is packed with a remarkable concentration of her work, and two particularly poignant features are the little summerhouse where she used to rest in

Tate Gallery

the afternoons, and the workshop which has been left entirely untouched since her death. Barbara Hepworth's studio is now administered by the ***Tate Gallery***, the London-based institution which has also opened a large-scale annexe in the town which is dedicated to the work of the St Ives School. An imposing white-painted building which uses Porthmeor Beach as a stunning backdrop, its architecture is thought by some to dwarf the quality of the work inside.

The narrow thoroughfares of St Ives contain an unusual number of museums and galleries. ***Penwith Galleries*** in Back Street West is a good place to see the work of the St Ives Society of Artists, a group founded by Sir Alfred Munnings. The ***St Ives Museum*** in Wheal Dream contains a unique collection of artefacts illustrating the natural, industrial and maritime history of the district, and includes a special feature on the exploits of John Knill. As a child, the writer Virginia Woolf spent most of her summers at Talland House overlooking St Ives Bay, from where it is possible to see the Godrevy lighthouse - the setting which provided the inspiration for her evocative and wonderful novel, *To the Lighthouse.*

A good way to travel to St Ives, especially in high summer when traffic congestion and parking can be a headache, is to park in ***St Erth*** or ***Leland*** and take the local train. The railway skirts St Ives Bay, with its five-mile long stretch of unbroken sand, and is widely regarded to be one of the loveliest coastal branch lines in Britain.

The train also passes close to ***Lelant Saltings***, a 500 acre tidal area at the mouth of the Hayle estuary which is now a RSPB bird sanctuary.

The eastern side of St Ives Bay is lined with one of the finest sandy beaches in Cornwall. A popular centre for windsurfing, various competitive events are staged here throughout the season, including breathtaking demonstrations of wave jumping.

The Count House is an impressive licensed hotel situated in a small quiet square and enjoying breathtaking views of the town, harbour and bay. Built from local granite in 1825, it takes its name from the fact that wages were counted out and paid from here to the tin miners of Wheal Trenwith. Each of the nine comfortable and stylish guestrooms is individually decorated - one features a four-poster and jacuzzi bath, while another has a distinctive canopied

The Count House

bed. There is also a cosy guests' lounge and well-stocked bar, which specialises in fine wines. The full English breakfast is a real treat; four-course evening meals also available upon request. All meals are home-prepared and home-cooked, and make use of the freshest local produce. Activities available locally include water-skiing, paragliding, windsurfing, fishing, pony-trekking and golf; sight-seeing trips around the bay to Seal Island are also on hand, as are excellent touring and walking along the coastal path. Open all year. *The Count House, Trenwith Square, St Ives, Cornwall TR26 1DJ Tel: 01736 795369.*

Around St Ives

Lelant

Map 1 ref F11

1½ miles SE of St Ives off the A30

Lelant was once an important port which lost out to St Ives when its anchorage became clogged with silt at the end of the Middle Ages. Now a flourishing holiday centre, its renowned golf links is overlooked by a 15th century church dedicated to St Uny, an early Celtic saint who is reputed to be the brother of Ia from St Ives. A spectacular view of St Ives Bay can be enjoyed from the summit of Trencrom Hill, the 500 foot granite prominence lying a mile and half west of Lelant. The site of a small Iron Age fort, excavations have revealed numerous hut circles and pottery fragments from the 2nd century BC. ***Merlin's Magic Land*** lying beside the A3074 between Lelant and Hayle offers a selection of popular fairground rides.

Hayle

Map 1 ref G11

2½ miles SE of St Ives off the A30

Hayle was a major industrial port and engineering centre in the centuries leading up to the decline of the mining industry at the turn of the 20th century. The great Cornish inventor, Richard Trevithick, built an early version of the steam locomotive here in the early 1800's, and not long after one of the first railways in the world was constructed to carry tin and copper to Hayle Quay from Redruth. At the height of the industry in the 19th century, steam-powered engines built by the famous *'Harveys of Hayle'* could be found in most of the mines in Cornwall. After more than a century of decline, plans have been drawn up to redevelop comprehensively the old port area.

Paradise Park can be found on the southern edge of Hayle. The park is a haven for rare and endangered birds, including the Cornish chough, a once-common inhabitant of the local cliffs which is now extinct in the county. (The striking red-billed bird is incorporated into the Cornish coat of arms.) Several species of brightly-plumaged parrots can be seen flying freely, and there is also an otter sanctuary where the animals are bred for possible re-introduction to the wild. Displays of eagles and other birds of prey in flight can be seen at certain times throughout the day.

Phillack

Map 1 ref G11

3 miles SE St Ives off the B3301

Here in this charming and once-flourishing port, ***The Bucket of Blood*** is an impressive and welcoming pub and restaurant with an intriguing history. Phillack predates its near neighbour Hayle as a renowned port, having traded with the ancient civilisations of Rome, Phoenicia and Scandinavia. There has been an inn on this site for

The Bucket of Blood Inn

hundreds of years, a haven for travellers, sailors, fishermen, miners and, it has to be said, pirates and smugglers. In those dark days, the innkeeper was one morning drawing water from the outside well - water which was used not just for the needs of the household but also in brewing the local strong, dark ale - when he found not water but blood in the bucket drawn up from the well. The resulting search discovered a corpse, identity unknown. The landlord and locals attest that the inn is haunted. The atmosphere in this charming pub - despite the presence of the ghost - is convivial and comfortable. The menu features steaks, chicken, pies, pasties and seafood, using locally available produce. *The Bucket of Blood Inn, 14 Church Town Road, Phillack, Hayle, Cornwall TR27 5AE Tel: 01736 752378*

Gwithian

Map 1 ref G11

4 miles E of St Ives off the B3301

This ancient village stands away from the tourist development behind the high windblown sand dunes, or towans, at the northern end of beach along the eastern side of St Ives Bay. This picturesque community of thatched cottages and farmhouses has a good inn, a tiny early 19th century cob-walled Methodist chapel, and a Victorian parish church with a low 15th century tower. The churchyard is filled with the graves of sailors who came to grief on nearby Godrevy Island. A sizable prehistoric settlement is said to lie buried beneath the nearby towans, along with a 7th century oratory founded by the Irish missionary, St Gothian. The stream passing between Gwithian and ***Godrevy Point*** is often stained with tin from the mines around Camborne, and is known appropriately as the Red river.

CHAPTER SIX
Southwest Cornwall & The Isles of Scilly

Minack Theatre, Porthcurno

Chapter 6 - Area Covered

For precise location of places please refer to the colour maps found at the rear of the book.

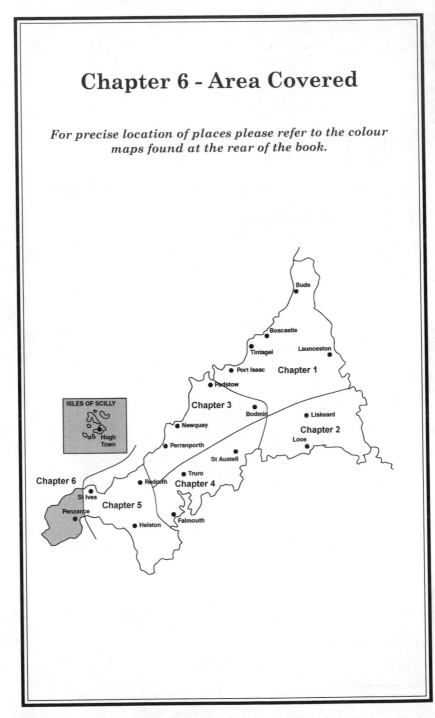

6
Southwest Cornwall & The Isles of Scilly

Introduction

This, the most southwesterly area of mainland Britain, juts out into the Atlantic and, as a result, experiences a mild climate with the help of the warm flowing waters of the Gulf stream. The southern coast, the *Cornish Riviera*, is characterised by small fishing harbours built in quiet natural coves and the strange village names of Marazion, Mousehole and Lamorna. Perhaps more than in any other region of Cornwall, legends and myths of exotic sea creatures, shipwrecks and smugglers abound. The great beauty and isolation of this wonderful part of the county has been an inspiration to many artists over the years - Newlyn, near Penzance, established itself as the base for a well-known school of artists at the beginning of the 20th century. The northern coast is the most rugged, wild and spectacular in the county. Here, bracken-covered and boulder-strewn moorland tumbles dramatically into the sea in a series of sharp headlands and rocky coves.

Penzance is the region's main town, has a bustling harbour, Cornwall's only promenade and much of historical interest as well as more modern-day amusements. A third of a mile offshore, and connected by a cobbled causeway which is exposed at low tide, ***St Michael's Mount*** is a remarkable granite outcrop which rises dramatically from the waters of Mount's Bay.

And what of Land's End, westernmost point of mainland Britain? Here, the granite backbone of West Penwith succumbs to the

Atlantic in a series of savage cliffs, reefs and sheer-sided islets, encompassing some awe-inspiring cliff scenery. Lying some 28 miles southwest, the *Avalon* of legend, where King Arthur is said to rest eternal: the Isles of Scilly, a granite archipelago of over 100 islands, of which only five are inhabited.

Penzance

Penzance is the principal town of West Penwith, lying in the northwestern corner of ***Mount's Bay***. For centuries, this was a remote market town which made its living from fishing, mining and smuggling. Along with nearby Newlyn and Mousehole, it was sacked by the Spanish in 1595, then at the end of the English Civil War it suffered a similar fate for being such a staunch supporter of the Royalist cause. However, the fortunes of the town were transformed by the arrival of the railway in 1859, a development which permitted the direct despatch of early flowers, vegetables and locally-caught fish to the urban centres of Britain, and which also allowed increasing numbers of holidaymakers to make the journey here easily. Today it is a bustling town and harbour, with Cornwall's only promenade.

The main, broad thoroughfare of Penzance, ***Market Jew Street***, takes its name from the Cornish term for *'Thursday market'*; it has a high stepped pavement on one side, and at its southwestern end there is a domed neoclassical ***Market House*** that was built in 1837. In front of this stands the statue of Penzance-born Humphry Davy, the 19th century scientists who is remembered for inventing the miners' safety lamp.

A number of interesting buildings are located in Chapel Street, a narrow thoroughfare which winds southwards from the Market House to the quay. The most unexpected of these is the ***Egyptian House***, with its exotic 1830's facade, which has been restored by the Landmark Trust; the National Trust occupy the ground-floor shop.

The Union Hotel opposite has an impressive Elizabethan interior which is concealed behind a Georgian frontage; the first mainland announcement of victory at Trafalgar and the death of Nelson was made from a minstrel's gallery in its main assembly room. At the rear stands the shell of one of the earliest theatres in the country, where performances were first held in 1787.

Further down Chapel Street there are two quaint old hostelries, the 13th century Turk's Head, and the Admiral Benbow Inn with its famous figure of a smuggler on the roof.

Almost facing the latter, the ***Maritime Museum*** contains a unique collection of artefacts recovered from shipwrecks around the Cornish coast. Marie Branwell, the mother of the Bronte sisters, was brought up at No 25 Chapel Street, and at its lower end the early 19th century St Mary's Church stands on a ledge above the harbour and Customs House, a reassuring landmark for returning sailors.

Elsewhere in Penzance there is an interesting ***Geological Museum*** in Alverton Street, a good local history museum and an exhibition of paintings by the Newlyn School in ***Penlee House Museum and Art Gallery***, and a striking collection of subtropical trees and flowers in ***Morrab Gardens***. The ***Aquarium and National Lighthouse Centre***, on the Quay, are also worth a look. The town is also a good stepping-off point for the ferry or helicopter to the Isles of Scilly.

Around Penzance

Gulval

Map 1 ref F12

1 mile N of Penzance off the B3311

The Coldstreamer Inn is an impressive gabled 19th century pub and restaurant in the charming village of Gulval, overlooking the fine village church and set amid lovely countryside, yet only three-quarters of a mile from the coast. Originally built to be a workhouse

The Coldstreamer Inn

and given to the village by commanding officers in the Coldstream Guards, which gives the pub its name, the main bar features a beamed and bare wood ceiling. The massive oak beams were brought in from local tin mines, and has an assortment of pews, Windsor chairs, carvers and stools for guests' comfort centred around the welcoming granite open fire.

The attractive restaurant features displays of military helmets, bugles, drums, flags and regimental memorabilia, complementing the exposed stonework and fine stained-pine panelling. There is an extensive selection of bar or main meals, with well over 20 main courses on offer. The two chefs use only the finest, freshest ingredients, including locally landed fish and seafood and marvellous local produce. The quiet, relaxed atmosphere in this warm and friendly establishment will enhance your enjoyment of your drink or meal. *The Coldstreamer Inn, Gulval, Penzance, Cornwall TR18 3BB Tel: 01736 362072.*

Long Rock *Map 1 ref F12*

1½ miles NE of Penzance off the A30

Mexico Inn is an imposing stonework Free House and restaurant offering real ales, excellent wines and an extensive menu featuring fresh locally landed fish, char-grilled steaks and vegetarian dishes, all home-made and home-prepared. Set near superb coastal scenery, this late-18th century pub was christened Mexico Inn by the tin mine workers for whom it was built. Then-owner Bill Trewar, a min-

Mexico Inn

ing engineer, had achieved success in silver mining in Mexico, and returned to Cornwall in 1794 to set up Long Rock Mine and obtained a beer licence in order to use the front parlour of his house as a public bar; he later purchased the adjoining cottage to extend the premises. The interior of this welcoming establishment boasts three distinct areas: the large main bar, the restaurant, and the snug. Each is decorated with an eclectic mix of traditional and modern comforts. Owners Bob and Jan Humpston are the warm and welcoming hosts; amiable and friendly, they make sure every guest is made to feel at home. *Mexico Inn, Long Rock, Penzance, Cornwall TR20 8JL Tel: 01736 710625.*

Marazion

Map 1 ref F12

3 miles NE of Penzance off the A394

It's well worth diverting off the A30 to visit Marazion, the ancient trading point on the mainland opposite St Michael's Mount. Cornwall's oldest charter town, Marazion was a port as long ago as the Bronze Age, and for many centuries this was the most important settlement on Mount's Bay. Its long history has left a legacy of fine old inns and residential buildings, and there is also a long sandy beach to the west which offers magnificent views of the Mount. ***Marazion Marsh***, on the inland side of the main road, is a protected breeding ground for many rare species of waterfowl. The town features a good stretch of sands, and a windsurfing centre.

St Michael's Mount

Map 1 ref F12

½ mile E of Penzance off the A30

A third of a mile offshore, and connected by a cobbled causeway which is exposed at low tide, St Michael's Mount is a remarkable granite outcrop which rises dramatically from the waters of Mount's Bay. The steep-sided islet has been inhabited by human beings since prehistoric times, and it has been a place of religious pilgrimage since a party of fisherman saw a vision of St Michael on the seaward side of the rock in the 8th century. Three centuries later, Edward the Confessor founded a priory here which was granted to the Benedictine monks of Mont St Michel in Normandy, the island's even more spectacular cousin across the Channel. The monastery was fortified after the Dissolution in 1539, and later passed to the St Aubyn family who incorporated the old monastic buildings into a series of 18th and 19th century improvements to form the striking multi-layered structure we can see today. A direct descendant of the family, Lord St Levan, donated the 21 acre site to the National Trust in 1954.

St Michael's Mount

The present-day structure contains some impressive medieval remains, most notably in the Chevy Chase room, the old chapel, and the central tower which soars to a height of over 250 feet above Mount's Bay. One of the relatively more recent additions is the southeast wing, which was designed in the 19th century by Piers St Aubyn, a cousin of the first Lord St Levan. The interior contains some fine period furniture, silver and paintings, including a number by St Agnes-born John Opie.

Newlyn

Map 1 ref F12

1½ miles SW of Penzance off the A30

An intriguing mixture of the elemental and the esoteric, the busy harbour of Newlyn, the largest fish-landing port in England and Wales, lies a short distance around Mount's Bay to the southwest of Penzance. Its massive jetties were built in the 1880's to enclose some 40 acres of the bay, including the existing 15th century harbour, to create the most important fishing port in the Southwest. This is now the base for around 200 vessels, varying in size from open lobster boats to large beam trawlers, whose valuable catches are shipped throughout Britain and Europe in huge refrigerated trucks.

But Newlyn also has another side: a highly regarded artistic tradition which was founded in the late 19th century by Stanhope

Forbes. The *'Newlyn School'* advanced the idea of working out of doors using everyday subjects in their natural light, and was a precursor to the school founded in St Ives in the first half of the 20th century. In 1895, the Cornish-born philanthropist, Passmore Edwards, presented the town with a splendid ***Art Gallery*** in New Road, and work by the many artists working in the area, along with those from much further afield, can be seen there to this day.

Another of Newlyn's attractions is ***The Pilchard Works***, a painstaking historical reproduction of the pilchard industry and the life and times of its workers.

Mousehole — *Map 1 ref F12*

2 miles SW of Penzance off the B3315

To the west of Penzance an outstanding circular route skirts the many beautiful coves and coastal communities of West Penwith. Mousehole (pronounced *Mouzel*) is one of the loveliest and most characteristic fishing villages in Cornwall. Along with Penzance, it was sacked by the Spanish in 1595, and subsequently rebuilt in solid Cornish granite. The parish churchyard at Paul, one mile inland, contains the grave of the fishwife, Dolly Pentreath, who was the last person in the county to speak only Cornish when she died in 1777. Injured and oil-covered seabirds are cared for at the ***Mousehole Wild Bird Hospital*** on Raginnis Hill; originally founded by the Yglesias sisters in 1928, it is still run by a private charity.

Every 23rd December, *'Star-Gazey'* pie, a local speciality with fish heads poking up through the pastry, is prepared in commemoration of the fisherman, Tom Bawcock, who saved Mousehole from starvation by setting sail in a storm and bringing home a large catch of fish. Less fortunate were the eight-man crew of the Penlee lifeboat, *Solomon Browne*, who were lost in hurricane conditions while attempting to rescue the last four crew members from the coaster Union Star in December, 1981; all were Mousehole men. The lifeboat station near Penlee Point has the steepest slipway in England.

At the end of a paved courtyard behind gates forged with stars and bronze fish, you will find ***The Millpool Gallery***, which features the works of several distinguished local artists, among them Nick Wilkinson, whose striking landscapes and seascapes were included at the 1995 *'Young Artists Exhibition'* at Bonhams in London, the same year his work was auctioned at the Royal Academy. He has also shown at the Royal West of England Academy and is a member of the Penzance Society of Artists. His pieces are undertaken on large canvases; he applies thin layers of paint to capture the unique qualities of light and shade that characterise the Cor-

The Millpool Gallery

nish landscape. His wife Jayne co-owns the gallery, which also showcases the work of several local craftspeople, including examples of driftwood furniture, decorated trinket boxes, wooden clocks fashioned by a local furniture maker, jewellery and knitwear - all of it unique and exquisitely crafted. If visitors would like to prolong their stay in this charming region of Cornwall, Nick and Jayne also have holiday accommodation available in a house with sea views and extensive gardens. *The Millpool Gallery, Mill Lane, Mousehole, Penzance, Cornwall TR19 6RP Tel: 01736 731115.*

Lamorna *Map 1 ref E13*

4 miles SW of Penzance off the B3315

This isolated granite hamlet is set in a craggy cove at the end of a beautiful wooded valley. Immortalised by artist Larmorna Birch, author Derek Tangye and in Cornish folk song, it makes for excellent walking along the small quay. Once only licensed to sell beer, Lamorna's pub, the ***'Wink'***, got its name from the old custom of winking to the landlord to obtain something stronger from under the counter.

An exceptional Bronze Age stone circle can be seen nearby, in a field beside the B3315. Known as the ***Merry Maidens***, its standing stones are reputed to be all that remains of 19 young women who were turned into granite for daring to dance on the Sabbath. The nearby ***'Pipers'***, two large menhirs 100 yards apart, are rumoured to be the accompanying musicians who suffered the same dire fate.

Liz Anderson is the able and cheerful owner of two self-catering holiday cottages here in Mousehole. ***Little Keigwin***, once part of a 16th-century manor house now divided into two, features handsome casement windows, beamed ceilings, exposed granite and a rough-rendered interior that speaks of its long and distinguished history. It features a groundfloor sitting/dining room, kitchen and double bedroom, and a huge upper-storey lounge with vaulted ceiling, bathroom and second double bedroom. ***Fairmaids*** offers pine furnishings in its capacious lounge and three bedrooms, two on the ground floor, one on the first. Both have supremely well-appointed kitchens, complete with dishwashers, microwaves, washing machines and a full complement of china, tableware and all the amenities guests have come to expect. With the sea only 50 metres away, Mousehole's superb and picturesque harbour and peaceful atmosphere make this an ideal base for exploring all the area has to offer: boating, fishing, driving, walking, garden spots, National Trust properties and a range of fine pubs and restaurants all found locally. *Liz Anderson, 'Bodriggy', Lamorna, Penzance, Cornwall TR19 6XW Tel/Fax: 01736 731206.*

Fairmaids

Treen *Map 1 ref E13*

6 miles SW of Penzance off the B3315

This ancient tin-streaming settlement shelters from the worst of the winter gales in a shallow valley in the lea of the clifftops. An attractive place with a good inn and campsite, the hamlet lies a short walk away from the spectacularly sited Iron Age coastal fort, ***Tretyn Dinas***. Despite having been constructed over 2,000 years ago, the earthwork defences on the landward side can still be made out. The distinctive arm of pinnacled granite at the opposite end of the headland incorporates the Logan (pronounced *Loggan*) Rock, a 65 ton boulder which at one time could be rocked by hand. The rock was a popular tourist attraction until 1824, when it was toppled into the sea by a group of naval ratings under the command of Lieutenant Hugh Goldsmith, the nephew of the poet and playwright Oliver Goldsmith. The officer was later instructed to replace the rock at his own expense, a task which turned out to require some extraordinary engineering skills, although sadly the fine balance of the rock stone was not restored. Details of the recovery operation can be found outside the inn.

Porthcurno *Map 1 ref D13*

6½ miles SW of Penzance off the B3315

One of the most dramatic and atmospheric coves in West Penwith, Porthcurno lies to the west of the Logan Rock. Reached by way of the coastal path or along a narrow and tortuous approach from the B3315, its exquisite white sand beach shelves into a turquoise sea between cliffs of weather-beaten granite. A number of undersea cables, including one running beneath the Atlantic, come ashore here.

The justly famous ***Minack Theatre*** stands perched on the headland overlooking the cove. Based on ancient Greek amphitheatres, this superb open-air auditorium was created in the early 1930's by

Minack Theatre

Rowena Cade. (It opened with an aptly chosen production of Shakespeare's *The Tempest* in 1932.) With its precariously positioned stage, rows of seating hewn from the rock, and azure backdrop of sea and sky, this must be one of the most spectacular theatre settings in the world. Performances take place from May through mid-September. Porthcurno is also home to the fascinating ***Museum of Wireless Telegraphy***.

St Levan

Map 1 ref D13

7 miles SW of Penzance off the B3315

This isolated hamlet has a handsome part-13th century parish church with a fine pinnacled tower, a simple Norman font, some unusual carved bench ends, and the remains of a 16th century painted rood screen.

In the churchyard can be seen the mass grave of the crew of the Liverpool-based grain ship Khyber, which ran aground on nearby rocks in 1905. There is also a tall pre-Norman cross and a curious twin boulder known as the ***St Levan's Stone*** which is said to have been split in two by the 6th century Celtic saint. St Levan is also reputed to have founded the now-roofless baptistery standing on the cliff above the secluded sandy beach of Porthchapel; water from the holy well is said to cure eye complaints, and is still used for baptisms. The superb stretch of the coastal footpath to the west takes in the lonely seaweed-strewn ***Porthgwarra Cove*** and the majestic cliffs around ***Gwennap Head*** on its way to the westernmost point in mainland Britain.

Land's End

Land's End is a curious mixture of natural spectacle and manmade indulgence. Here, the granite backbone of West Penwith succumbs to the Atlantic in a series of savage cliffs, reefs and sheer-sided islets, encompassing some awe-inspiring cliff scenery. On a clear day it is possible to see beyond the ***Longships*** (a mile and a half offshore) and the ***Wolf Rock*** (7 miles offshore) lighthouses to the Isles of Scilly, over 25 miles away to the southwest.

The Land's End site, mainland Britain's most westerly point, has long been in private hands and, over the years, various attempts have been made to create a visitor attraction worthy of this illustrious setting. The ***'Land's End Experience'*** heritage centre offers a range of impressive audio-visual presentations on the natural and maritime history of the area, which since Roman times has been known as the *'Seat of Storms'*. There is also a hotel with magnificent sea views, and a number of children's attractions.

The Land's End airport is situated beside the B3306 to the north-east of Whitesand Bay; as well as a regular service to the Isles of Scilly, short flights can be taken which offer visitors a spectacular bird's-eye view of the surrounding coastline.

Around Land's End

Sennen — *Map 1 ref D12*

1 mile E of Land's End off the A30

Sennen's 15th century church is the most westerly in mainland Britain. The wide sandy Blue Flag beach at ***Sennen Cove*** offers some excellent bathing and surfing. A lifeboat slip has been stationed here since 1853, and today a modern rescue vessel continues to serve one of the most perilous stretches of coastline in the British Isles. The former windlass house is now a crafts gallery. From here visitors can indulge in excellent cliff walks to Land's End.

Here in world-famous Land's End and opposite the handsome St Sennen's Church, ***Old Manor Hotel*** offers gracious and very comfortable hospitality in its eight beautifully appointed guest bedrooms. Located amid beautiful cliff-side, seacoast and upland moor scenery and the sandy beach at nearby Sennen, this 18th century hotel retains a wealth of original features, including blackened beamed ceilings in the bedrooms, oak panelling, fine architraving and coving,

The Old Manor Hotel

and several wonderful fireplaces, including one of polished marble in the restaurant and an enormous granite one in the snug, complete with bench seat inside. The low doorways, unusual stained glass window on the staircase and former servants' stairway complete the charming and cosy ambience of this unique hotel. Morning coffee, lunch, cream teas and evening meals are available, offering a well-balanced choice of traditional meals and vegetarian dishes, all home-made. Daytrips by air are available from nearby Land's End Airport to the Isles of Scilly and for sightseeing excursions. *Old Manor Hotel, Sennen, Land's End, Cornwall TR19 7AD Tel: 01736 871280.*

St Just

Map 1 ref D12

4 miles NE of Land's End off the B3306

St Just stands at the southwestern margin of one of the most remarkable areas of industrial archeology in the country. An austere community of low granite houses and inns, this was once an important tin- and copper-mining centre. Despite the demise of the industry, the streets still have a solemn working air: there are two Methodist chapels, one with a neoclassical facade and room for almost 100 worshippers, and a solid 15th century church which contains some fascinating early relics, including two medieval wall paintings, now restored, and a 5th or 6th century headstone carved with a faint inscription from the dawn of British Christianity. A shallow grassy amphitheatre can be found near the clock tower in the centre of town; known as ***'Plen-an-Gwary'***, it was once used for performing medieval miracle plays and is now a venue for an annual carnival. There is a convenient Skybus from here to the Isles of Scilly.

Cape Cornwall

Map 1 ref D12

4½ miles NE of Land's End off the B3306

Often referred to as the only cape in England, the National Trust-owned Cape Cornwall marks the supposed boundary between the English and St George's Channels. The chimney on the summit came from the former Cape Cornwall mine, abandoned in 1870. This is fine walking country; offshore, Brisons reef holds the macabre record for most shipwrecks.

Botallack

Map 1 ref D11

5½ miles NE of Land's End off the B3306

On the cliffs near Botallack can be seen a pair of the most spectacularly sited old ***Crown Tin Mine Engine Houses*** in Cornwall.

Reached via the coastal footpath or along a track from the village, these partly restored industrial relics once delivered the workforce to, and removed material from, a network of tin mines which reached out far beneath the waves. (During severe storms, miners were said to have been able to hear the movement of boulders on the seabed above them.) According to tradition, the Cornish pasty was developed by local tin-mining families as an easy and relatively hygienic way of providing cooked food for consumption underground.

Trewellard

Map 1 ref D11

6 miles NE of Land's End off the B3306

An ***engine house*** here in Trewellard contains the oldest working beam engine, restored by the National Trust. The Levant mine was the scene of a tragic accident in 1919 when the mechanism for raising miners to the surface catastrophically failed, killing 31 men and boys. Visitors are now able to see the engine in operation after it had lain unused for over 60 years.

Pendeen

Map 1 ref D11

6½ miles NE of Land's End off the B3306

Geevor Tin Mine and Heritage Centre, the last of the 20 or so mines in the area to close, can be seen beside the main road in Pendeen. A lane to the north of the village leads to the strikingly situated lighthouse on ***Pendeen Watch***, which is open to the public on most fine days.

Zennor

Map 1 ref E11

5 miles NE of St Just on the B3306

The 9 mile stretch of coastline between Pendeen Watch and St Ives is among the wildest and most spectacular in Cornwall. Here, bracken-covered and boulder-strewn moorland tumbles dramatically into the sea in a series of sharp headlands and rocky coves. Zennor is one of the few settlements in this stark landscape. An ancient village skirted by the coast road which has a history dating back to the early Bronze Age, its 12th century ***church of St Senara*** contains a wooden bench known as the Mermaid's chair, which was made around 500 years ago from two carved bench ends.

One side of this chair depicts the figure of a mermaid holding a mirror and comb and which resembles depictions of Aphrodite, the Greek goddess of love. A famous local legend tells of a mysterious young maiden who was drawn to the church by the beautiful singing voice of the squire's son, Matthew Trewhella. An enchanting singer herself, one night she lured him down to nearby Pendour

Cove (now known as ***Mermaid's Cove***) where he swam out to join her and disappeared. On a warm summer's evening some say their voices can be heard rising from beneath the waves. The village also has a fine old inn, the Tinner's Arms, and an informative local museum, ***Wayside Folk Museum***, which gives some interesting background information on this most fascinating part of West Cornwall.

Further inland, the granite moorland of West Penwith is littered with a remarkable number of prehistoric remains. A mile to the southeast of Zennor village, ***Zennor Quoit*** is a Neolithic chamber tomb whose huge capstone was once supported on five broad uprights; two other standing stones mark the entrance to an inner chamber.

Gurnards Head Hotel is set amid beautiful scenery near lovely coastal walks and sandy beaches. The four guest rooms are supremely comfortable. Built in the 1830's of local granite, this imposing establishment also boasts an excellent restaurant, its menu featuring fresh local produce and locally landed fish and seafood, all home-prepared and home-cooked. The atmosphere in this charming and welcoming hotel is relaxed and friendly; owners Ray and Joy Kell have brought their 26 years of experience to ensuring guests' every comfort and convenience. The service and efficiency offered by them and their staff are of the highest standard.

The large beer garden is the perfect place to enjoy a quiet drink, amid some truly tranquil and relaxing surroundings. The immediate area offers many opportunities to indulge in watersports, walking, sightseeing and all the delights that St Ives, Zennor and the surrounding region have to offer. Guests return again and again

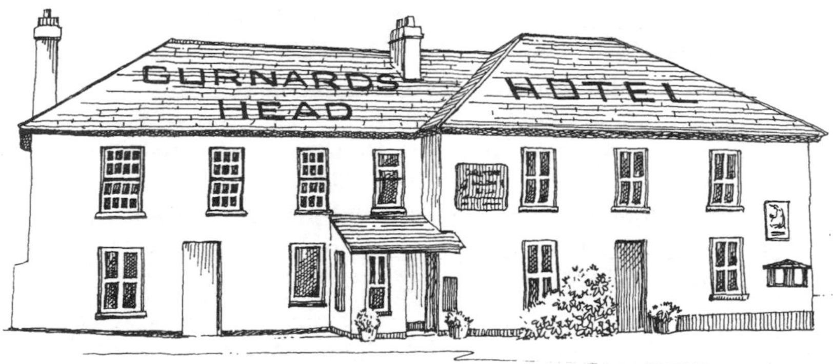

Gurnards Head Hotel

to this charming and attractive hotel. *Gurnards Head Hotel, Treen, Zennor, St Ives, Cornwall TR26 3DE Tel: 01736 796928.*

Chysauster *Map 1 ref F11*

2 miles SE of Zennor off the B3306

Chysauster is one of the best-preserved Iron Age settlements in southern Britain, lying on an exposed hillside in the heart of the Penwith peninsula. Founded around 100 BC, this ancient village was occupied for around four centuries. It then lay undisturbed for over 1,500 years until archeological excavations in the 1860's revealed a sizable grouping of nine courtyard houses arranged on either side of a central thoroughfare. The village is adjoined by an irregular pattern of small Iron Age fields, and also incorporates the remains of a fogou, a semi-underground stone-lined trench which would probably have been used for storing communally-owned provisions.

Half a mile east, the ground rises onto the 750 foot hill occupied by the Iron Age fort, ***Castle-an-Dinas***. Its still discernible system of defensive ditches and stone ramparts are centred upon a folly of the late 18th century; from here there are marvellous views over west Cornwall. Further west, and reached along a narrow road which runs between Morvah and Mandron, is ***Lanyan Quoit***, a remarkable 5,000 year-old Neolithic chamber tomb which looks like a massive three-legged stone table. The 13 ton capstone was re-erected in Victorian times with the help of lifting gear that was used to replace the Logan stone near Treen. According to legend, King Arthur ate his last meal here before going into his final battle.

To the south of Lanyon Quoit, the road passes close by the ***Holy Well of St Madernus***, another place which is claimed to have healing powers. It's an ancient custom for those making a wish here to tie a piece of cloth onto a branch which overhangs the water. Nearby there is a roofless baptistery with a tiny stone altar.

A mile and a half north, a rough track leads to the mysterious ***Men-an-Tol***, a holed stone standing between two menhirs. Probably Bronze Age in origin, it is said to have curative powers which can relieve a range of conditions from backache and rickets to infertility and impotence. Other Iron Age chamber tombs in the area include ***Chun Quoit*** near Morvah, and ***Mufra Quoit*** near New Mill.

Madron *Map 1 ref E12*

4 miles S of Zennor off the B3311

The part 14th century church here in Madron was once the mother church of Penzance; inside there is a fine wagon roof, a Norman font and a 17th century monumental brass to a former mayor of Penzance, as well as a Trafalgar Banner, celebrating Nelson's victory.

The National Trust-owned ***Trengwainton Garden*** lies on the southwestern edge of the village; it is particularly known for its large spring-flowering shrubs, walled garden and fine views of Mount's Bay. The moorlands on the outskirts of town are rich in antiquities, including the ***Maen Scryfa*** inscribed stone.

Grumbla

Map 1 ref E12

5 miles SW of Zennor off the A3071

The Iron Age fort of Caer Bran can be reached along a footpath from this tiny hamlet.

Sancreed

Map 1 ref E12

6 miles SW of Zennor off the A3071

Several very interesting prehistoric sites can be found around this ancient village. Two Bronze Age monuments, the ***Blind Fiddler*** and the ***Two Sisters***, stand within a quarter-mile of each other behind the hedge on the northern side of the Land's End road. Like many Cornish menhirs, they are said to represent human beings turned to stone for committing irreligious acts on the Sabbath.

Brane

Map 1 ref E12

6½ miles SW of Zennor off the A30

Half a mile west and above this lovely hamlet, the fascinating Iron Age courtyard village of ***Carn Euny***, founded around 300 BC by an early Cornish farming community, is renowned for having the best preserved granite-lined fogou in Britain. This mysterious 65 foot long underground passage leads to a circular chamber which may have been used for purposes of religion, storage or habitation.

Isles of Scilly

Lying approximately 28 miles southwest of Land's End, the Scillies are a granite archipelago of over 100 islands, of which only five are inhabited: St Mary's, Tresco, St Martin's, St Agnes and Bryher. Legend has it that this was *Lyonesse*, or the last remnant remaining above the waves, as well as *Avalon*, to which the bier of King Arthur was sorrowfully transported.

The islanders' traditional occupations of fishing, boat building and smuggling have given them a fierce sense of independence from both Cornwall and the rest of Britain. However, in recent decades the economy has grown more and more dependent on the income from visitors as increasing numbers fly in from Penzance, Newquay and St Just, or arrive aboard the ferry from Penzance.

Most come to escape from the pressures of modern living (there are very few cars on the islands, and only 9 miles of drivable road), to visit some of the 100 or so Bronze Age sites, to observe migrating birds, or simply to enjoy the unique flora which thrive in this exceptionally mild climate. A good time to visit is during the flower harvest in early spring, a busy season which culminates in an annual flower show in March. The origin of the Scillies' flower industry is believed to go back to 1867, when a local farmer sent some early blooms to Covent Garden in his aunt's hat box. The industry was later encouraged by Augustus Smith, the benevolent landlord who administered the islands in the mid-19th century.

St Mary's — *Map 1 ref B16*

St Mary's, the main island, is the first port of call for most visitors. Most arrive at the small air terminal at Old Town, or step ashore in the harbour in Hugh Town, the main centre of population which stands on a narrow isthmus between the *'mainland'* and the Garrison peninsula on the island's southwestern corner. A pleasant walk around the peninsula takes in a number of gun emplacements dating from the time the island was fortified against possible Spanish aggression in the 1590s. ***Star Castle*** was built during this era in the shape of an eight-pointed star (it is now a hotel), and the Garrison, with its imposing gateway, was completed 150 years later. The peninsula is an excellent place from which to view the other islands and the sun setting over the Atlantic.

The ***Isles of Scilly Museum*** in Hugh Town has a variety of interesting displays on the archeology, natural and maritime history of the islands. One of its central features is a fully-rigged pilot gig, a forerunner of the modern open rowing boats which take part in spectacular races around the islands during the summer months.

Elsewhere on St Mary's there are numerous beaches and interesting geological formations, particularly around Peninnis Head, the southernmost point on the island. At ***Porth Hellick Bay*** to the east, a huge rock stands as a memorial to Sir Cloudesley Shovell, the unfortunate admiral whose flagship, the Association, and three other warships ran aground on the Western Rocks in October 1707, with the loss of around 2,000 men - the most calamitous of the islands' many shipwrecks.

A group of five ancient chambered tombs stand above the bay on

Porth Hellick Down. Similar examples can be found at the northern end of the island at ***Innisidgen Carn*** and ***Bant's Carn***; the latter is also the site of an Iron Age settlement.

Turnerstone Gifts is a delighful and charming shop situated in Hugh Street on St Mary's island, right in the middle of town. The building dates back to the 18th century, and was once home to the Isles of Scilly Electrical Supply Company. These small, cosy and interesting premises are filled with intriguing and unique gifts and crafts. Owners Ian and Rose Tabraham have run this thriving concern together here for the past five years; they are welcoming and informative proprietors, who make every effort to ensure that visitors can make the best possible choice from among their many and

Turnerstone Gifts

handsome exquisitely crafted wares. Die-cast models are an unexpected speciality in a shop which features the work of local craftsmen, artists and artisans; pottery, paintings and other artwork, as well as unique greetings cards and postcards produced from Ian's photographs, plants and bulbs, and charming souvenirs of the Scillies. Visitors will want to take some of these unique crafts and other mementoes home with them, to remind them of this wonderful part of the world. *Turnerstone Gifts, Hugh Street, St Mary's. Isles of Scilly TR21 0LL Tel: 01720 422733*

April Cottage is a charming and extensive family-run guest house, situated in a tranquil spot close to the parish church on St Mary's island. It is very convenient for the quay and the many attractive shops and restaurants on the island and has a lovely garden which guests are welcome to enjoy. The bedrooms (all en suite) are furnished to a high standard, with pretty details and en eye towards guests' every comfort and convenience. Every room has a TV, radio and tea/coffee-making facilities; hair dryer and iron are available on request. The guests lounge and conservatory are the perfect place to enjoy some peaceful relaxation in cosy and convivial surroundings and are open to guests at all times.

April Cottage

Proprietor Mrs Janet House and her daughter Mrs Louise Hicks make every effort to help guests feel comfortable and at home and take particular pride in the hearty full English breakfast on offer, which should set guests up for the day! April Cottage is a non-smoking establishment The St Mary's Boatmens Association provides a comprehensive boating service in season including circular trips out to see the seals and local birdlife. This service leaves the quay at 10.15 in the morning and 2.00 in the afternoon, tides and weather permitting. Evening fishing trips (in season) and fishing boat charter hire are also available. Whether you arrive by sea or air, a warm welcome in peaceful surroundings awaits you at this delightful establishment. *April Cottage, Church Road, St Mary's, Isles of Scilly TR21 0NA Tel: 01720 422279 Fax: 01720 423247*

Tresco

Map 1 ref B15

The inter-island ferry departs from St Mary's quay at regular intervals throughout the day. A crossing to Tresco provides an opportunity to observe some of the island's abundant wildlife, including puffins and Atlantic grey seals.

Tresco's internationally renowned ***Abbey Botanical Gardens*** were planted in the 1830s by Augustus Smith in the grounds of a ruined 10th century Benedictine priory.

Begun as a small collection of plants from Kew, specimens from all over the world have gradually been added to create one of the finest subtropical gardens in the world. Augustus Smith also established the ***Valhalla Figurehead Museum*** within the grounds of the Abbey Gardens, a unique collection of figureheads and other artefacts salvaged from ships wrecked off the Scillies.

St Martins

Map 1 ref C15

St Martin's island, the third largest of the Scillies, is peaceful, picturesque and renowned for its beautiful white sandy beaches, which are safe for bathing. Sailing and diving tuition are available on the island. Birdwatching walks are a regular popular event, as are boat trips to view the local wildlife. Pleasure launches leave daily for the other Isles of Scilly; fishing trips can also bearranged. Two evenings a week there's the opportunity to follow the inter-island gig-boat raceing. The islands Village Hall (known as the Reading Room) has indoor games facilities, for which temporary membership is available. St Martin's also features an outdoor tennis court and a local cricket team, happy to take on a *'visitors eleven'* every week in summer.

St Martin's Campsite on the island is a small fanily-run site which offers excellent facilities and good service. The site is ideally situated, being sheltered, mainly flat and adjacent to a beautiful south-facing beach. The site has a modern facility block which was built with the aid of the British Tourist Board and meets the Board's exacting standards; there are flush-toilets, wash-basins with free hot and cold water, coin operated showers and hair-driers and basins for laundry and dishashing. Drinking water is available from standpipes on the site.

On a recent West Country Tourist Board inspection the campsite was awarded theree ticks in the National Quality Scheme - an official endorsement of the high standards to be found here. No camping equipment is provided but manager Chris Savill and his wife and

St Martin's Campsite

staff can provide visitors with Calor gas, Camping gas, paraffin, methylated spirits and various small gas cartridges. Fresh milk, eggs and seasonal vegetablesare available in most instances from their farm. St Martin's Island has a post office/general stores and a greengrocer/ delicatessan so most provisions are on hand for anyone staying at the campsite. Orders sent to the Savills in advance can be ready for your arrival. Meals and snacks can also be taken at the local tearooms, pub and hotel. Transport can be arranged for camping equipment to and from St Martin'squay. (please note no dogs are allowed on the site.) All the facilities and the marvellous feeling of being *'far from the madding crowd'* make St Martin's campsite a perferct choice for a relaxing getaway. *St Martin's Campsite, Middle Town, St Martin's, Isles of Scilly TR25 0QN Tel: 01720 422888*

St Agnes

Map 1 ref B16

The whitewashed lighthouse on St Agnes is one of the earliest examples of its kind in the British Isles; now disused, it still serves as an effective mariners' daymark. Elsewhere on St Agnes, and on the other two inhabited islands, ***St Martin's*** and ***Bryher***, there are fine sandy beaches and some interesting prehistoric remains. The western island of ***Annet*** is a sanctuary for seabirds - landing is not permitted during the breeding season.

Tourist Information Centres

Centres in **bold** are open all the year around.

Bodmin

Shire House, Mount Folly Square, Bodmin, Cornwall PL31 2DQ
Tel/Fax: 01208 76616

Bude

The Crescent, Bude, Cornwall EX23 8LE
Tel: 01288 354240, Fax: 01288 355769

Camelford

The North Cornwall Museum, The Clease, Camelford Cornwall PL32 9PL Tel/Fax: 01840 212954

Falmouth

28 Killigrew Street, Falmouth, Cornwall TR11 3PN
Tel: 01326 312300, Fax: 01326 313457

Fowey

The Post Office, 4 Custom House Hill, Fowey, Cornwall PL23 1AA
Tel/Fax: 01726 833616

Helston & The Lizard Peninsula

79 Meneage Street, Helston, Cornwall TR12 8RB
Tel: 01326 565431, Fax: 01326 572803

Isles of Scilly

Porthcressa Bank, St Mary's, Isles of Scilly, Cornwall TR21 0JL
Tel: 01720 422536, Fax: 01720 422049

Launceston

Market House Arcade, Market Street, Launceston
Cornwall PL15 8EP Tel: 01566 772321, Fax: 01566 772322

Looe

The Guildhall, Fore Street, East Looe, Cornwall PL13 1AA
Tel: 01503 262076, Fax: 01503 265426

Newquay

Municipal Offices, Marcus Hill, Newquay, Cornwall TR7 1BD
Tel: 01637 871345, Fax: 01637 852025

Padstow

Red Brick Building, North Quay, PAdstow, Cornwall PL28 8AF
Tel: 01841 533449, Fax: 01841 532356

Penzance

Station Road, Penzance, Cornwall TR18 2NF
Tel: 01736 362207, Fax: 01736 363600

St Ives

The Guildhall, Street-an-Pol, St Ives, Cornwall TR26 2DS
Tel: 01736 796297, Fax: 01736 798309

Truro

Municipal Buildings, Boscawen Street, Truro
Cornwall TR12 2NE Tel: 01872 274555

Wadebridge

The Town Hall, Wadebridge, Cornwall PL27 7AQ
Tel: 01208 813725

Index

A

B

C

D

E

F

G

H

I

J

K

L

M

N

O

P

Q

R

S

U

V

W

Z

The Hidden Places Series

ORDER FORM

To order more copies of this title or any of the others in this series please complete the order form below and send to:

Travel Publishing Ltd,7a Apollo House, Calleva Park Aldermaston, Berkshire, RG7 8TN

	Price	Quantity	Value
Regional Titles			
Channel Islands	£6.99	....	....
Cheshire	£7.99	....	....
Cornwall	£7.99	....	....
Devon	£7.99	....	....
Dorset, Hants & Isle of Wight	£4.95	....	....
East Anglia	£4.95	....	....
Gloucestershire	£6.99	....	....
Heart of England	£4.95	....	....
Kent	£7.99	....	....
Lancashire	£7.99	....	....
Lake District & Cumbria	£7.99	....	....
Northeast Yorkshire	£6.99	....	....
Northumberland & Durham	£6.99	....	....
Nottinghamshire	£6.99	....	....
Peak District	£6.99	....	....
Potteries	£6.99	....	....
Somerset	£6.99	....	....
South East	£4.95	....	....
South Wales	£4.95	....	....
Surrey	£6.99	....	....
Sussex	£6.99	....	....
Thames & Chilterns	£5.99	....	....
Welsh Borders	£5.99	....	....
Wiltshire	£6.99	....	....
Yorkshire Dales	£6.99	....	....
Set of any 5 Regional titles	**£25.00**	....	....
National Titles			
England	£9.99	....	....
Ireland	£8.99	....	....
Scotland	£8.99	....	....
Wales	£8.99	....	....
Set of all 4 National titles	**£28.00**	....	....
	TOTAL	______	______

For orders of less than 4 copies please add £1 per book for postage & packing. Orders over 4 copies P & P free.

PLEASE TURN OVER TO COMPLETE PAYMENT DETAILS

The Hidden Places Series
ORDER FORM

Please complete following details:

I wish to pay for this order by:

Cheque:	☐	Switch:	☐
Access:	☐	Visa:	☐

Either:

Card No: ☐☐☐☐ ☐☐☐☐ ☐☐☐☐ ☐☐☐☐

Expiry Date: ☐☐ ☐☐

Signature: ....

Or:

I enclose a cheque for £ .... made payable to Travel Publishing Ltd

NAME: ....

ADDRESS: ....

....

....

....

POSTCODE: ....

TEL NO: ....

Please send to: Travel Publishing Ltd
7a Apollo House
Calleva Park
Aldermaston
Berkshire, RG7 8TN

The Hidden Places Series

READER REACTION FORM

The Hidden Places research team would like to receive reader's comments on any visitor attractions or places reviewed in the book and also recommendations for suitable entries to be included in the next edition. This will help ensure that the ***Hidden Places*** series continues to provide its readers with useful information on the more interesting, unusual or unique features of each attraction or place ensuring that their stay in the local area is an enjoyable and stimulating experience.

To provide your comments or recommendations would you please complete the forms below as indicated and send to: **The Research Department, Travel Publishing Ltd., 7a Apollo House, Calleva Park, Aldermaston, Reading, RG7 8TN.**

Please tick as appropriate: Comments ☐ Recommendation ☐

Name of *"Hidden Place"*:

Address:

Telephone Number:

Name of Contact:

Comments/Reason for recommendation:

Name of Reader:

Address:

Telephone Number:

The Hidden Places Series

READER REACTION FORM

The Hidden Places research team would like to receive reader's comments on any visitor attractions or places reviewed in the book and also recommendations for suitable entries to be included in the next edition. This will help ensure that the ***Hidden Places*** series continues to provide its readers with useful information on the more interesting, unusual or unique features of each attraction or place ensuring that their stay in the local area is an enjoyable and stimulating experience.

To provide your comments or recommendations would you please complete the forms below as indicated and send to: **The Research Department, Travel Publishing Ltd., 7a Apollo House, Calleva Park, Aldermaston, Reading, RG7 8TN.**

Please tick as appropriate: Comments ☐ Recommendation ☐

Name of *"Hidden Place"*:

Address:

Telephone Number:

Name of Contact:

Comments/Reason for recommendation:

Name of Reader:

Address:

Telephone Number:

Map Section

The following pages of maps encompass the main cities, towns and geographical features of Cornwall, as well as all the many interesting places featured in the guide. Distances are indicated by the use of scale bars located below each of the maps

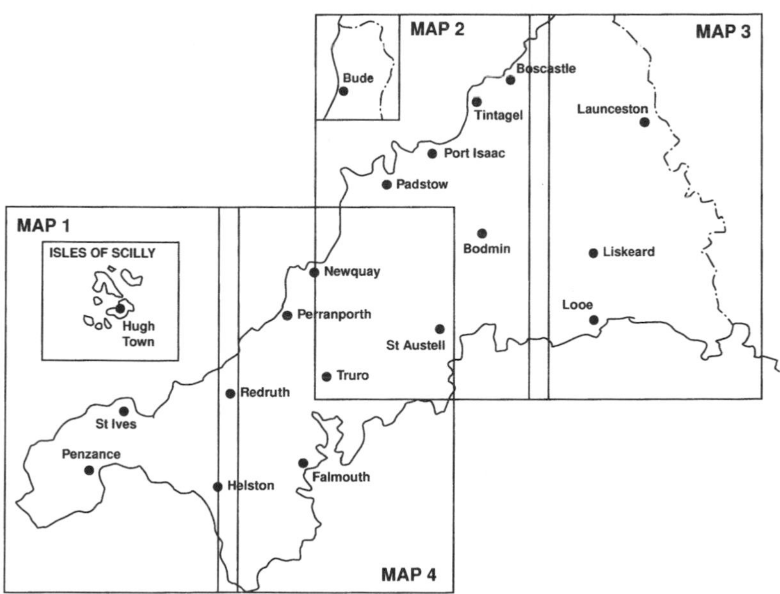

These maps are small scale extracts from the *Devon and Cornwall Tourist Map,* reproduced with kind permission of *Estates Publications.*